JAMES JOYCE

THE *FINNEGANS WAKE* NOTEBOOKS AT BUFFALO

Notebook VI.B.25

Editors: Vincent Deane,
Daniel Ferrer, Geert Lernout

Introduction: Vincent Deane
Bibliographic description: Luca Crispi

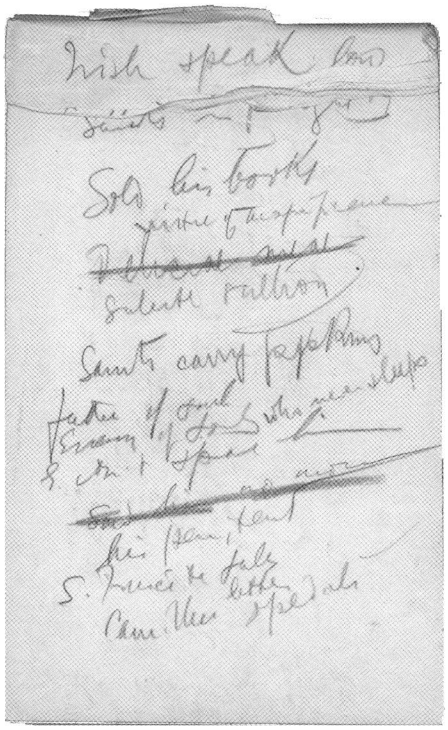

BREPOLS PUBLISHERS

Publication of this volume was assisted by
The Baird Foundation, Buffalo, New York; Francis G. Church Fund, Buffalo, New York;
The Office of the Provost, University at Buffalo, The State University of New York;
Institut des Textes et Manuscrits Modernes (CNRS); The University of Antwerp.

D/2002/0095/107

ISBN 2-503-51352-2

Table of Contents

INTRODUCTION TO VI.B.25

Description

VI.B.25 belongs to the early group of notebooks, VI.B.10-VI.B.1. These are all stenographer's jotters with pages that flip up so that the writing on each verso is upside down in relation to the preceding recto. Like the others it was manufactured for short-term use, so it is of poor quality. In addition it has been badly mutilated. In its present condition traces of 96 leaves remain: the original total was probably 100. Only 13 leaves survive intact: the remainder consists of stubs on many of which fragments of the original inscriptions can be read.

Date of Compilation

In 1966, Jack Dalton commented on the discrepancy between the relatively late number assigned to this notebook by Spielberg and its proper place in the chronological sequence which, considering its use in the 'Kevin' episode, he judged to be early.[1] Earliest draft use was the basis for Roland McHugh's attempt to provide a more accurate chronology for all of the notebooks: he gave VI.B.25 a time-span of August-October 1923.[2] Further confirmation of an early date is indicated by the absence of the character symbols commonly known as sigla (the markings at the end of page 168 are later additions) and by the dramatis personae. The dominant characters are still Kevin, Tristan and Issy, whose names appear in a variety of forms; Pop, who had first emerged in VI.B.3, appears twice and Patrick appears once as 'SP' and possibly a second time as 'Pat the Man' (see 'Selective List of Sources and Topics' for examples). At 155*b* and 156*c* appear the first notes relating to Finn's Hotel. Is it possible, in spite of their undeniable personal associations, that these were at first suggested by some newspaper article or advertisement? Both instances are surrounded by material of this kind. The identified newspaper sources themselves provide a further refinement of the dating, as they range from 25 June (023*a*) to early August 1923 (162*c*, *i*): although the source for the note on Doggett's Coat and Badge, the annual Thames boat race, at 153*k*, has not been specifically located, the race itself was held on 1 August. All of this points to July to August as the period of compilation, the time of Joyce's visit to Bognor, an aspect which is reflected in the surviving fragmentary notes on pages 030-1, taken from the Ward Lock Guide to that Sussex resort, which will be discussed later in this introduction.

The two character symbols mentioned above, Λc Δ , are inscribed in red crayon on page 168. They stand for *FW* III.3 and I.8, to which Joyce transferred a number of units from VI.B.25, cancelled in red. David Hayman, in his introduction to the *Archive* reproduction of VI.B.25, has suggested that these must have been added after the destruction of the notebook.[3] This statement is corroborated by the fact that 168 is the last intact page of the notebook as it stands. The same two symbols, also inscribed in red crayon, can be seen on the back cover of VI.B.16, which was also used in the composition of III.3 and I.8, often in the same drafts as the VI.B.25 transfers.

Joyce devised the code consisting of the Shaun symbol combined with the first four letters of the alphabet in order to indicate the four episodes of Book III, the 'Four Watches of Shaun'. It makes its first appearance in mid-1925 on VI.B.9.145, so already we can say that the signs were added some time after the drafts of I.8 and III.3 (mid to late 1924) for which the notebook was used. Joyce's purpose in marking his notebooks in this way seems to have been to enable him to tell at a glance the predominant thematic function of the contents. Besides the symbols other kinds of labeling were used to assign notebooks to groups relating to their usage: place names, such as Nice or Zurich, or a 't' followed by a number, to indicate an issue of *transition*.

We need not suppose that all of the notebooks were marked at one specific period, but it does seem reasonable to imagine that, when Joyce hit on the idea of adding identifying labels to his notebooks, he

---

[1] Jack P. Dalton, 'Advertisement For the Restoration', *Twelve and a Tilly: Essays on the Occasion of the 25th Anniversary of 'Finnegans Wake'*, ed. Jack P. Dalton and Clive Hart (Evanston: Northwestern University Press, 1966), 119-37.

[2] Roland McHugh, 'Chronology of the Buffalo Notebooks', *A Wake Newslitter* 9 (April 1972): 27.

[3] *JJA* 35:xi.

would mark all or most of the notebooks that he had accumulated up to this point. If we accept that VI.B.25 and VI.B.16 were marked at the same time, it would seem highly likely that the very similar VI.B.10, VI.B.3 and VI.B.6 would also have been given distinctive markings. In the case of VI.B.3, page 001 has the inscription 'Z'ch' (i.e. Zurich) in orange. VI.B.21 and VI.B.33 have similar orange inscriptions: 'Z'ch 33' (i.e. Zurich, 1933) and 'Zurich Feldkirch' respectively. All of this suggests an overall date for this batch of labels, of sometime around 1933, when Mme Raphael began to copy uncrossed material from the B notebooks into those notebooks we now know as the C series.

The inscriptions for all three notebooks appear at the beginning and indeed it makes most sense to add identifying symbols to the beginning or end of a notebook, if it has a cover, or—if the cover is missing—to an outer page, where the inscription can be found with the minimum of effort. The related issue of the mutilation of VI.B.25 will be discussed later in greater detail, under the heading of 'VI.A Transfers'. At this stage the labeling suggests a terminus ad quem of c.1933.

Nature of the Notes

Notetaking in VI.B.25 combines aspects of its two predecessors: the apparently random selections from newspaper articles and periodicals typical of VI.B.10 are to be found alongside the more purposeful-looking extracts from books, first seen in VI.B.3. Although, given the damaged condition of the notebook, it is difficult to be certain, it seems likely that here (as in later notebooks in this sequence) Joyce had already turned from the *Irish Times* to the *Freeman's Journal*—some of the surviving notes have been taken from its daily column, 'By the Way'. This was a banner for a number of short anecdotal features, often just a paragraph in length, on topics that sometimes had a bearing on the news of the day, but that were more often dictated solely by the anonymous writer's inclination. In this way it has a function similar to that of the *Daily Mail* articles, which provided similarly diverse tidbits of information for VI.B.10. There is also continuity in Joyce's return (not for the last time) to the belligerently nationalistic *Leader*, although the notes here (167*g-i*) are untypically mild.

VI.A Transfers

In his preface to the drafts of *FW* II.2 in the *James Joyce Archive*, David Hayman suggested *en passant* that those pages of 'Scribbledehobble' (VI.A, 1-47) used in the composition of II.2§4.*0 might in turn have been taken from missing pages of VI.B.25.[4] Some sixteen years later this was shown to be the case by Jorn Barger in an article examining transfers from three of the earliest notebooks to VI.A.[5] In the following table are listed all of the transfers identified so far, of which traces still remain in the original notebook. In three cases (023*a*, 027*a*, 133*a*) decipherment of the VI.B.25 note was only practicable because of its VI.A counterpart (this also made it possible to find a source for 023*a*, which in turn further clarified the reading for both notebooks).

VI.B.25	**VI.A**
009(a) Irish speak low	0031 ('An Encounter'): I speak low
013(a) S Kevin's Chapel—Pro Cathedral Dublin	0032 S ('An Encounter'): Kevin's Chapel Procathedral
023(a) Gingerbread built *[??]* Dominick	0034 ('An Encounter'): John Whislton built / Gingerbread
027(a) no more tay for / *[??]* th*[??]*	0034 ('An Encounter'): no more tay for sugar the cosey
028(a) */*bath*]* *[??]*	?0040 ('An Encounter'): bath copper
133(a) *[*croo*]* ked stick & grey goose *[??]*	0044 ('Araby'): crooked stick & grey goose quill
143(f) Saints carry pipkins	0045 ('Araby'): saint carry pipkin
144(c) Monsignor Kevin	0045 ('Araby'): Mgr Kevin
157(i) sulkies	0041 ('Araby'): sulkies

[4] *JJA* 52:x.

[5] Jorn Barger. 'A Preliminary Stratigraphy of "Scribbledehobble"', *'Finnegans Wake': Teems of Times*, ed. Andrew Treip (Amsterdam: Rodopi, 1994), 127-37.

One question that naturally arises at this point is whether there is a connection between the VI.B.25 transfers and the state of the notebook. Barger, for example, seems to think there is and goes even further, suggesting that a similar process on a smaller scale would account for missing pages in VI.B.10 and VI.B.3 as well.[6] This is to make a number of assumptions: that Joyce was himself responsible for the present state of VI.B.25; that he chose to damage it; and that the mutilation served a creative purpose.

Regarding the first two, the likelihood of this scenario would depend on the plausibility of the action as a means to an end. In fact Barger seems to be suggesting two scenarios, each with its own rationale. In the first he suggests that Joyce may have devised a basic blueprint for his new book, which he wanted to conceal; in the second he seems to be accounting for the destruction as a means of avoiding reduplication of the transferred items.

The first hypothesis is highly problematic on a number of fronts. All the evidence seems to indicate that Joyce was still far from having a plan when he was entering material into VI.B.25. Joyce's development of the various plots involving HCE and family in Book One seems to depend more at this stage on his brilliant gift for transforming material encountered by chance in newspapers than on any hidden plan. But even if we grant that there was such a schema, would it necessitate the removal of more than one hundred pages? The plans we do have are terse, usually taking the form of diagrams, or tables of properties: the *Ulysses* Linati schema, for example, or the plan of the verses at the end of *FW* Book II, or the map of Waterloo for the Museyroom scene. All of these are eminently practical, easy to consult; clearly setting out the essentials on one side of a piece of paper (they were also plans Joyce was pleased to make available). The longer and more detailed a plan becomes the less useful it is likely to be as a plan (although it may have evolved at this stage into something even more useful—an actual draft). It might also be asked why Joyce would want to destroy his schema anyway? If it were short, he could probably easily remember it (but then it would not account for so many missing pages), but if it were long and complex he would surely want to keep it at least until he had finished his book. Besides, who would be likely to read his notebooks unless so directed by him?

The second hypothesis, that the tearing was connected with the transference of units, would seem to envisage the process as an alternative to colour strikethroughs. This also raises some hard questions. Joyce uses his crayons to cross any item that he transfers into a draft, but he does not apply this method to material transferred between notebooks, whether from the B notebooks to VI.A, or from B notebook to B notebook, or from B notebook to C notebook (in the latter case cancellation might have saved Mme Raphael some unnecessary reduplication). As Barger himself has so usefully demonstrated, the handful of units transferred to VI.A from VI.B.10 and VI.B.3 is still very visible in these notebooks: Joyce does not seem to have attempted to mark this material in any way.

But the most difficult aspect of the hypothesis that the destruction of VI.B.25 was purposive would be the sheer unwieldiness of the process. After all, in his use of colours, Joyce had already devised an excellent method for channeling large quantities of extremely diverse data, which allowed him to transfer lexical units at random: as many or as few as he wanted, at any given moment, from one page to another. With tearing as a method this control is lost: the process cannot be used to transfer a single unit somewhere in the middle of a page of notes, nor can one discriminate between recto or verso. The transference of any single item would entail an attack on two pages.

There is also the question of when these latter transfers might have been made. Danis Rose, in his introduction to VI.A in the *Archive* suggests 1926 as the date for these D entries,[7] but in the *Textual Diaries* he has pushed it forward to early March 1931.[8] This is in part based on first draft use (early drafts of *FW* II.1), but it also seems to find confirmation in a letter from Joyce to Miss Weaver, dated 11 March 1931, in which he tells her: 'I take up some of my daughter-in-law's time trying to copy into one large book the worst of my illegibly scrawled notes.'[9] The date of this letter seems a likely terminus a quo for

[6] *Op. cit.,* 134-5. No distinction seems to be made here between the VI.B.25 transfers in handwriting D and those from VI.B.10 in handwriting A.

[7] *JJA* 28:xxvii.

[8] *Op. cit.,* 31.

[9] *Letters* I, 303.

the destruction of the notebook (which would necessarily follow the transfers). The original 1926 date for these entries was based on the assumption that the handwriting D entries on page 746 of VI.A were used in *FW* I.1, which was drafted in this year, whereas, as Rose later concluded, these items were in fact *derived from* that text by Joyce as a means of establishing thematic continuity.[10]

Reconstructing Missing Units

It is possible to deduce by various means a number of other missing units. For example, a VI.B.25 source of which only a few units survive in the notebook itself, but which was clearly used in drafts composed around the time of other notebook-to-draft transfers; or a source known to have been in Joyce's possession at the time he was compiling VI.B.25, units from which may be found in VI.A and in the *FW* drafts. The sections that follow explore these possibilities in greater detail.

The Ward Lock Guide

This valuable source was discovered by Peter Timmerman, who wrote a perceptive account of it in *A 'Wake' Newslitter*.[11] Only two notes from the *Guide*, each taken from a short section on fishing near the beginning, survive in the present notebook (030*b*, 031*a*). Timmermann demonstrated that Joyce had used a number of other units in the same section of the *Wake*, nearly all of them in the same draft. There can be little doubt that these were entered onto missing pages of VI.B.25. Taking them in the order in which they occur in the *Guide*, they are as follows:

Marine Hotel

Guide to Bognor 'Hotel, Boarding House […] Directory' 6: Selsey, near Chichester. / The Marine Hotel / only hotel on sea front.
MS 47472-97, TMA: ~~like~~ ^+Like+^ Cincinnatus ~~he~~ ^+the G. O. G. (grand old gardiner)+^ was one ^+sabbath+^ day ~~at~~ ^+following+^ his plough ^+for rootles+^ ^+in the rear garden of his Royal Marine Hotel+^ | *JJA* 45:002 | Aug-Sep 1923 | I.2§1.*0 | *FW* 030.16

Lobster traps

Guide to Bognor 21: At the entrance to the Pier, and at other spots on the Parade, are numbers of the— / Wicker Traps, or "Pots," / in which lobsters, crabs and prawns are taken. These traps are made by the fishermen.
MS 47472-98, ILS: ~~inquiring~~ ^+~~??~~ ^+asking to be put wise+^+^ whether ~~he had not been engaged in~~ ^+ ~~whitebait~~ ^+paternoster+^ were not now more fancied ^+bait+^ for+^ lobster trapping | *JJA* 45:004 | Aug-Sep 1923 | I.2§1.*1 | *FW* 031.07

Hundred of Manhood

Guide to Bognor 'Chichester' 54: **The Selsey Tramway.** From Chichester to Selsey Hill runs a light railway called the Hundred of Manhood and Selsey Tramway.
MS 47472-97, TMA: ^+and discarding finally those theories which would link him either with the Glues & Gravys & Earwickers of Sidlesham ^+in the hundred of manhood+^+^ | *JJA* 45:002 | Aug-Sep 1923 | I.2§1.*0 | *FW* 030.08

Sidlesham / Earwicker, Glue, Gravy, >

MS 47472-97, TMA: ^+and discarding finally those theories which would link him either with the Glues & Gravys & Earwickers of Sidlesham […]+^ | *JJA* 45:002 | Aug-Sep 1923 | I.2§1.*0 | *FW* 030.06-8

Boniface >

Anker, and Northeast.

Guide to Bognor 'Chichester' 54: Sidlesham Church is an Early English structure worthy of notice, and an examination of the surrounding tombstones should not be omitted if any interest is felt in deciphering curious names, striking examples being Earwicker, Glue, Gravy, Boniface, Anker, and Northeast.

---

[10] See Michael Groden, '*Ulysses*' *in Progress* (Princeton, New Jersey: Princeton University Press, 1977), 196-200 for a discussion of similar procedures in the composition of *Ulysses*.

[11] Peter Timmerman, 'The First Guide to *Finnegans* Wake', *A Wake Newslitter* 16 (June 1979): 45-8.

MS 47472-102, TsILA: the Glues, the Gravys ^+the Northeasts, the Ankers+^ and the Earwickers | *JJA* 45:014 | Spring 1925 | I.2§1.3 | *FW* 030.07

The Proverbs of Wales

In an unpublished letter in the British Library dated 4 July 1923 (MS 57347-72), Miss Weaver tells Joyce that she has sent him T.R. Roberts' *The Proverbs of Wales* along with a catalogue of plays. Joyce had just arrived in Bognor at this date, so the package could hardly have taken more than a day to reach him

As can be seen from a number of other notes scattered through the surviving pages of VI.B.25 (133*a*, 142*a*, 165*a*), the Roberts book was part of a more general interest of Joyce's in proverbs at this period. *The Proverbs of Wales* consists of a short introduction, followed by some nine hundred alphabetically-listed proverbs in Welsh, with interlinear English translations. Beyond some prefatory generalisations, Roberts provides no commentary on his collection nor does he attempt to place the more individual items in a historical context. As the proverbs themselves consist for the most part of trite admonitions such as 'Let him who reads reflect' or 'Polluted are the perjured lips', the book makes for fairly dull reading—any reader looking for more of the sort of colourful phrases that Joyce has found will be sorely disappointed. Several of these can be seen, in handwriting D, on pages 37-8 of VI.A, under the heading 'An Encounter'.[12] These were almost certainly taken from the pages of VI.B.25. The order of these VI.A notes, unlike the earlier transfers in handwriting A, is not random, but preserves the original order of the source, and presumably of the VI.B.25 notes. The process referred to in Joyce's letter quoted above was not a sorting exercise, but rather a forerunner of the Raphael transfers: no further items appear under other headings in VI.A. A few more of Roberts' proverbs can be found in the pages of the *Wake*, to which they were almost certainly transferred, from missing pages of VI.B.25. Like the Bognor notes these are also given here in the order in which they are to be found in the source text. In this case no attempt has been made to reconstruct the notes as they would have been identical to the source citations.

Proverbs of Wales 18: I know milk though I am not used to it.
MS 47481-17, their ~~favourite proverb~~ ^+orthodox proverb+^ that ^+old+^ fellow knows milk though he's not used to it | *JJA* 56:051 | Oct 1923 | II.4§2.*2 FW 390.27-8

Proverbs of Wales 27: Seek the nest of evil in the bosom of a good word.
47471b-69v, Seeker of ^+the nest ^+of+^+^ evil in the bosom of a good word | JJA 47:384 | Jan-Feb 1924 | I.7§2*1 | *FW* 189.28

Proverbs of Wales 59: The butter is in the cow's horns (that is, when she gives no milk).
47471b-12v, I'll go bail like the bull of the Cow / All your butter is / in your horns JJA 45:040 | Oct-Nov 1923 | I.2§3.*0 | *FW* 045.23

Proverbs of Wales 86: In the bird's lodging (to spend the night under a hedge).
47482b-30, I'd ask no kinder fate than to stay where I am this moment ^+in the bird's lodging [...]+^ | *JJA* 57:061 | May 1924 | III§1A.*2/1D.*2//2A.*2/2C*2 | *FW* 449.17

Moore's Melodies

Pages 158-9 contain the earliest record of an extended foray into Moore's emblematic *Irish Melodies*.[13] Joyce would return to this source a number of times in the course of the *Wake*, sometimes desultorily adding allusions to the work in progress, but it is only in the final years of composition that he adopts the completist approach that characterises the published text of his book. Although he must have been able to sing a great many of the *Melodies* from memory, it is interesting to note that the list here has obviously been carefully compiled from a printed copy: see for example 158*g-i*, which have been

---

[12] See Vincent Deane and Roland McHugh, 'Robert's *Proverbs of Wales*', *A Finnegans Wake Circular* 4.2 (1988): 32-5, for a transcription of these. I no longer hold the view expressed there that the non-notebook units were transferred straight from the source.
[13] For a discussion of the VI.B.25 Moore notes in the context of later notebooks, see Danis Rose, John O'Hanlon and Vincent Deane, 'Moore at the *Wake*', *A Finnegans Wake Circular* 5 (1989-1990): 1-40.

transcribed from a footnote to 'Though the last glimpse of Erin'. Although a few clear allusions appear among the notes, many of the phrases collected here (such as those from the footnote) hardly function as reminiscences. They were largely used in the 'Tristan and Isolde' episode, which they help imbue with faded drawingroom diction. Joyce's approach here makes missing units less easy to identify. The most likely candidate is to be found in the 'Kevin' episode:

> *Moore's Melodies:* The Meeting of the Waters (air: The Old Head of Denis).
> MS 47488-25, ILA: amiddle of the ^+meeting waters of+^ river Slaney and Liffey river | *JJA* 63:038c | Jul 1923 | IV§2.*2 | *FW* 605.12

Irish and Religious

The Finn's Hotel references are the nearest we have to personal notes amid the debris. A number of Irish references can still be made out, including two casual mentions of Chapelizod, at 011 (its drill band remains unidentified at the time of writing) and 025. We also have notes on the Irish tricolour (019*a*), the Vigilance Committee (033*a*), Sinn Féin (107*a*), Tim Healy (141*a*), and the Ulster border (150*e*). The range of other topics covered, even in this small number of surviving pages, can be seen by looking at the 'Selective List of Sources and Topics'.

The most extensive remaining category is religion. As the Ward Lock guide is associated with HCE and the Moore's *Melodies* with Tristan and Isolde, so this last set of material was collected largely for use in drafts of the Kevin episode. The most unified and purposeful under this heading are to be found on 172, 174, 176 and 178. Here we find a series of lists, often numerologically significant, of evangelical counsels, liturgical colours, canonical hours, most of them transferred to IV§2. But this draft also incorporated several other theological lists which were almost certainly transferred from missing notebook pages. Prominent among these are the ninefold celestial hierarchies, the seven sacraments and the seven orders of priesthood discussed by Dalton, which are to be found already incorporated into the main body of the draft.[14] In a book which gives such a prominent role to clothing, it is perhaps surprising that Joyce did not also bestow on Kevin the array of priestly vestments worn during the mass. Among the interlinear additions to the draft, 'alb' is the sole indication that VI.B.25 might have contained such a list.

It seems very likely that the following units, which ring further changes on 'create', were inscribed on the missing portion of page 178:

increate / creator

> *Note:* Increate. Not created—said of God.
> MS 47488-25, LMA: of Kevin of ^+increate+^ God the servant of the Lord Creator | *JJA* 63:038c | July 1923 | IV§2.*2 | *FW* 000.00

procreate

> MS 47488-25, LMA: ^+procreated+^ on the ^+ultimate+^ island of Ireland | *JJA* 63:038c | July 1923 | IV§2.*2 | *FW* 605.04

recreate

> MS 47488-25, LMA: ^+recreated+^ doctor solitarius, Keeper of the door of meditation, he ^+recreated+^ meditates | *JJA* 63:038c | July 1923 | IV§2.*2 | *FW* 605.07

cocreate

> MS 47488-25, ILS: letting there be water where before was dry land having ~~created~~ ^+cocreated+^ which | *JJA* 63:038c | July 1923 | IV§2.*2 | [*FW* 605.35]

The following terms are also likely to have appeared on an adjacent page:

---

[14] Dalton, *Op. cit.*, 120.

triune / Trishagion

Note: Triune. Constituting a trinity in unity, used with reference to God and the Trinity.

Trishagion, or Trisagion. A hymn in the early church addressing God thrice as holy.

MS 47488-25, LMA: piously Kevin ^+lauding the Triune Trishagion+^ amidships of his conducible altar super bath | *JJA* 63:038c | July 1923 | IV§2.*2 | *FW* 605.14

Draft Usage.

Possibly because material had already been transferred to VI.A, possibly because of its by then damaged state, the uncancelled VI.B.25 units were not copied by Mme Raphael. The chief usage seems to have taken place between the time of its compilation, July to August 1923, and the early drafts of I.I, at the end of 1926, when items were transferred to all chapters composed within this duration. As we have seen above, particular use of it was made in adding to the early 'Kevin' and 'Tristan' episodes. Its most important contribution however was to the evolution of 'Pop' into HCE, by means of the Ward Lock notes.

While it is to be regretted that more of VI.B.25 has not survived it is possible to deduce a surprising amount from what remains and it is very likely that a full account of the drafts in which it was used, together with discovery of the relevant sources, will allow us in time to account for much more of what is missing.

Vincent Deane
Dublin, 2002

Acknowledgements

Louise Clarke, Lowestoft Record Office and Mike Sims, Lowestoft, for information on the Roman Hill School (145*n*).

Source Identification

A Pictorial and Descriptive Guide to Bognor located by Peter Timmerman. See *A Wake Newslitter* 16 (June 1979): 45-8.

East Sussex Place Names (154*g*) located by Geert Lernout.

All other source material located by Vincent Deane.

Source Bibliography

A Pictorial and Descriptive Guide to Bognor, Chichester, Selsey … etc. (London: Ward, Lock and Co., Ltd., 1922-1923).

Moore, Thomas. *Moore's Irish Melodies* (edition unknown).

General Bibliography

Barger, Jorn. 'A Preliminary Stratigraphy of "Scribbledehobble"', '*Finnegans Wake': Teems of Times*, Andrew Treip ed. (Amsterdam: Rodopi, 1994): 127-137.

Connolly, Thomas E., ed. *James Joyce's Scribbledehobble: The Ur-Workbook for 'Finnegans Wake.'* (Evanston: Northwestern University Press, 1961).

Dalton, Jack P. 'Advertisement For the Restoration', *Twelve and a Tilly: Essays on the Occasion of the 25th Anniversary of 'Finnegans Wake*', Jack P. Dalton and Clive Hart eds. (Evanston: Northwestern University Press, 1966): 119-137.

Deane, Vincent and McHugh Roland. 'Robert's *Proverbs of Wales', A Finnegans Wake Circular* 4.2 (1988): 32-35.

Dermod, McCarthy. *Saint Mary's Pro-Cathedral* (Dublin: Eason & Son Ltd.,1988).

Groden, Michael, ed. *The James Joyce Archive,* Volume 35, Prefaced and Arranged By Danis Rose; Volume 52, Prefaced by David Hayman and Arranged by Danis Rose with the Assistance of John O'Hanlon (New York and London: Garland Publishing, 1978).

Hayman, David. *A First-Draft Version of 'Finnegans Wake.*' (Austin: University of Texas Press, 1963).

—. ' "Scribbledehobbles" and How They Grew', *Twelve and a Tilly: Essays on the Occasion of the 25th Anniversary of 'Finnegans Wake*', Jack P. Dalton and Clive Hart eds. (Evanston: Northwestern University Press, 1966): 107-118.

—. 'Notebook VI.B.25', *JJA* 35:xi-xii.

—. *The 'Wake' in Transit* (Ithaca: Cornell University Press, 1990).

—. 'Transiting the *Wake*: a Response to Danis Rose,' *JJQ* 29.2 (1991): 411-419.

Hutchins, Patricia. *James Joyce's World* (London: Methuan and Co. Ltd, 1957).

McHugh Roland. 'Chronology of the Buffalo Notebooks', *A Wake Newslitter* 9.2 (1972): 19-31; 9.3 (1972).

—. 'A Structural Theory of *Finnegans Wake* Revisited', *A Wake Newslitter* 13.5 (1976): 94-95.

—. *The Sigla of 'Finnegans Wake*' (London: Edward Arnold, 1976).

Rose, Danis. 'The Beginning of all Thisorder of Work in Progress,' *JJQ* 28.4 (1990): 957-965. [A review of Hayman's *The 'Wake' in Transit.*]

—. *The Textual Diaries of James Joyce* (Dublin: Lilliput Press, 1995).

—, John O'Hanlon and Vincent Deane, 'Moore at the "*Wake*"', *A Finnegans Wake Circular* 5 (1989-1990): 1-40.

Spielberg, Peter. *James Joyce's Manuscripts and Letters at the University of Buffalo: A Catalogue.* (Buffalo: University of Buffalo, 1962).

Bibliographic Description[1]

Material: The MS. is a tablet and Joyce's handwriting is in lead pencil. The notebook is similar in kind to the six other extant notebooks of the period (October 1922–April 1924), all of which have horizontal spines: MSS. VI.B.10, B.3, B.2, B.11, B.6 and B.1 Joyce used red, blue, orange, brown and green coloured crayons to cross through notes as he harvested them for use in his manuscripts.[2]

Collation: The MS. consists of 96 leaves of unruled, refined, pulp paper (although most likely some further leaves are no longer extant). Only 13 leaves (26 pages: 143–68) survive intact, except for a tear in the top corner of most pages; most are fully inscribed and none are completely blank. The remaining 83 leaves (166 pages) survive only as fragments of various dimensions, of which 50 pages retain notes of at least one line or partial words and phrases (pp. 009-19, 021, 023, 025, 027-31, 033-8, 105, 107-9, 113, 115, 118-20, 123, 124, 126, 128, 129, 131, 133, 136, 137, 139, 141, 142, 172, 174, 176, 178, and 184); 24 pages retain unintelligible portions of letters and/or words (pp. 008, 020, 032, 039, 041, 045, 047, 055-7, 065, 111, 112, 114, 117, 121, 122, 125, 127, 132, 134, 135, 140, and 184). On the other hand, 64 pages appear blank, but are small enough to make it impossible to ascertain whether they had been inscribed (pp. 001-6, 040, 042-4, 046, 048-54, 058-64, 066-104, 169 and 170); and 26 appear blank but are large enough to suggest that they may not have been inscribed (pp. 007, 022, 024, 026, 106, 110, 116, 130, 138, 171, 173, 175, 177, 179, 180-3, and 185-92). The sheets were stapled twice in the centre and folded in half horizontally to form the tablet. The notebook has *no* covers. The MS. was dis-bound for preservation purposes and analysis in July 2001.

Pagination: The pages are *unnumbered*. The pages as numbered in the *JJA* do not correspond to the actual state of the manuscript:

Notebook Page:	*JJA* Pagination:
001-008	000
009-038	001-030
039-104	000
105-168	031-094
169-170	000
171-8	095-102
179-192	000

Measurements: The MS. measures 21.2 x 13.2 cm. (as trimmed), although the fragments that survive differ in size (see the following chart).

---

[1] For previous bibliographic description of the manuscript see Bernard Gheerbrant, *James Joyce: Sa Vie, Son Œuvre, Son Rayonnement* (Paris: La Hune, 1949), item 157; John J. Slocum and Herbert Calhoon, A *Bibliography of James Joyce 1882-1941* (New Haven: Yale University Press, 1953), item E.7.b, p. 147; and Peter Spielberg *James Joyce's Manuscripts and Letters at the University of Buffalo: A Catalogue* (Buffalo: University of Buffalo, 1962), 114.

[2] Based on the evidence available at present, it is not possible to determine objectively whether Joyce used one or more different red coloured crayons in this MS. The differences in the apparently various shades of red may be due to the crayon(s), the manner in which Joyce used the crayon(s) or to a combination of these factors. In terms of draft usage, no distinguishing pattern emerged to differentiate between the shades of red. Therefore, they have not been distinguished here.

Other Markings: Traces of the colour crayon from the cross through markings appear on pp. 138 and 175, as well as on ten further, smaller pages (pp. 48 and 49, 66 and 67, 72 and 73, 76 and 77, 80 and 81), suggesting that either one of the facing pages may have been inscribed. Joyce wrote "Λc Δ" (up-side down) in red crayon on p. 168.[3]

Publication: Page 009-38, 105-68 and 171-8 of the MS. have been reproduced in black and white photo-facsimile in *JJA* 35:002-025.

Notes: The state of the manuscript as it survives indicates that pages were unevenly torn in clusters from the notebook by hand: of the extant torn pages almost 75% were from the front of the notebook, but only 12.5% from the back. Remnants around the staples are all that remain of 8 leaves (16 pages: 89-104), these 4 sheets were pulled from the centre of the notebook.[4] It is not clear why the notebook was taken apart in the manner it was, why the notebook was preserved in its present state, nor if it was Joyce himself who destroyed the notebook.

Although only a small portion of this MS. survives, enough evidence remains to speculate about its prior state. The notebook was presumably still intact in March 1931, when Joyce transferred some of its notes sequentially (at least through the extant pages) to MS. VI.A.0031-44. He habitually used notebooks composed of sheets that were bound with horizontal spines as though the two adjoined pages formed one page. That is, when the notebook was fully opened, Joyce would inscribe even numbered pages from what was physically their top edge towards the centre spine, continuing to take notes on the facing, odd numbered pages from the centre spine towards what was physically the bottom edge of these notebook pages. Therefore, presumably (at least) the even numbered pages 008-20, 028-38, 056, 108, 112, 114, 118, 120, 132-6, 140-50, 156 and possibly 184 were inscribed with notes to the bottom edge. Based on the manner in which Joyce typically used this type of notebook, all of the notes inscribed on pp. 153, 154, 158 and 159, 161, 163, 164 and 165, 166 and 167, 168, 172, 174, 176, 178, and 184 are upside down, as are some of those on pp. 152, 155, 160, 162. This pattern of inscription suggests that Joyce compiled this notebook both from front to back and back to front. Correspondingly, if Joyce inscribed the latter portion of the notebook consistently upside down (if at all), then the odd numbered pages 169, 173-9 and 185 may have been inscribed. Not enough remains of the odd numbered pages 179-92 to be sure if those were inscribed upside down (if at all).

Luca Crispi
The Poetry/Rare Books Collection,
University Libraries,
University at Buffalo,
The State University of New York

---

[3] Joyce labeled all of the extant early notebooks, VI.B.10-B.19, with similar sigla markings, on either the front or the back, presumably to indicate their prior use. VI.B.16 was likewise tagged "Λc" (III.3) and "Δ" (I.8) on its back cover, presumably at the same time as B.25. Presumably more or less contemporaneously with the labeling of B.25 (that is, mid-1925 through 1933), VI.B.1 and B.14 were also tagged "Λc"; B.10, B.3 B.2, B.11, B.6, and B.5 were tagged "Δ"; and analogous Book III sigla labels were made on VI.B10, B.2, B.11, B.6, B.1, B.5, B.14, VI.D.3 and D.2 (that is, VI.C.5.091 and C.15.025), B.9, B.8, and B.19.

[4] MS VI.B.10 was similarly dismantled, although the staples here remained closed.

Measurements of Individual Pages:

Page	Measurement:
001	0.9 x 5.5 cm.
002	0.9 x 5.5 cm.
003	0.9 x 5.8 cm.
004	0.9 x 5.8 cm.
005	0.5 x 5.7 cm.
006	0.5 x 5.7 cm.
007	1.1 x 8.3 cm.
008	1.1 x 8.3 cm.
009	3.0 x 13.0 cm.
010	3.0 x 13.0 cm.
011	3.2 x 13.2 cm.
012	3.2 x 13.2 cm.
013	3.2 x 13.2 cm.
014	3.2 x 13.2 cm.
015	3.3 x 13.2 cm.
016	3.3 x 13.2 cm.
017	2.7 x 13.2 cm.
018	2.7 x 13.2 cm.
019	2.6 x 13.2 cm.
020	2.6 x 13.2 cm.
021	2.6 x 13.2 cm.
022	2.6 x 13.2 cm.
023	2.6 x 13.2 cm.
024	2.6 x 13.2 cm.
025	2.6 x 13.2 cm.
026	2.6 x 13.2 cm.
027	2.6 x 13.2 cm.
028	2.6 x 13.2 cm.
029	2.6 x 13.2 cm.
030	2.6 x 13.2 cm.
031	2.6 x 13.2 cm.
032	2.6 x 13.2 cm.
033	2.6 x 13.2 cm.
034	2.6 x 13.2 cm.
035	2.6 x 13.2 cm.
036	2.6 x 13.2 cm.
037	2.6 x 13.2 cm.
038	2.6 x 13.2 cm.
039	0.7 x 12.9 cm.
040	0.7 x 12.9 cm.
041	0.7 x 12.5 cm.
042	0.7 x 12.5 cm.
043	0.7 x 12.5 cm.
044	0.7 x 12.5 cm.
045	0.6 x 10.5 cm.
046	0.6 x 10.5 cm.
047	0.6 x 10.5 cm.
048	0.6 x 10.5 cm.
049	0.5 x 9.0 cm.
050	0.5 x 9.0 cm.
051	0.5 x 7.2 cm.
052	0.5 x 7.2 cm.
053	0.5 x 6.6 cm.
054	0.5 x 6.6 cm.
055	0.5 x 6.6 cm.
056	0.5 x 6.6 cm.
057	0.5 x 6.6 cm.
058	0.5 x 6.6 cm.
059	0.5 x 6.6 cm.
060	0.5 x 6.6 cm.
061	0.5 x 6.6 cm.
062	0.5 x 6.6 cm.
063	0.5 x 6.6 cm.
064	0.5 x 6.6 cm.
065	0.4 x 4.5 cm.
066	0.4 x 4.5 cm.
067	0.3 x 4.0 cm.
068	0.3 x 4.0 cm.
069	0.3 x 3.9 cm.
070	0.3 x 3.9 cm.
071	0.3 x 3.7 cm.
072	0.3 x 3.7 cm.
073	0.3 x 3.7 cm.
074	0.3 x 3.7 cm.
075	0.2 x 2.0 cm.
076	0.2 x 2.0 cm.
077	0.2 x 2.0 cm.
078	0.2 x 2.0 cm.
079	0.2 x 1.5 cm.
080	0.2 x 1.5 cm.
081	0.1 x 1.0 cm.
082	0.1 x 1.0 cm.
083	0.0 x 9.0 cm.
084	0.0 x 0.5 cm.
085	0.0 x 0.5 cm.
086	0.0 x 0.5 cm.
087	0.0 x 0.5 cm.
088	0.0 x 0.5 cm.
089	0.5 x 1.6 cm.
090	0.5 x 1.6 cm.
091	0.5 x 1.6 cm.
092	0.5 x 1.6 cm.
093	0.5 x 1.6 cm.
094	0.5 x 1.6 cm.
095	0.5 x 1.6 cm.

096	0.5 x 1.6 cm.
097	0.5 x 1.6 cm.
098	0.5 x 1.6 cm.
099	0.5 x 1.6 cm.
100	0.5 x 1.6 cm.
101	0.5 x 1.6 cm.
102	0.5 x 1.6 cm.
103	0.5 x 1.6 cm.
104	0.1 x 1.6 cm.
105	2.0 x 9.0 cm.
106	2.0 x 9.0 cm.
107	2.0 x 9.0 cm.
108	2.0 x 9.0 cm.
109	2.0 x 9.0 cm.
110	2.0 x 9.0 cm.
111	2.0 x 8.4 cm.
112	2.0 x 8.4 cm.
113	2.0 x 8.5 cm.
114	2.0 x 8.5 cm.
115	2.1 x 9.0 cm.
116	2.1 x 9.0 cm.
117	2.0 x 9.0 cm.
118	2.0 x 9.0 cm.
119	2.0 x 8.7 cm.
120	2.0 x 8.7 cm.
121	2.0 x 8.5 cm.
122	2.0 x 8.5 cm.
123	2.1 x 9.2 cm.
124	2.1 x 9.2 cm.
125	2.1 x 9.5 cm.
126	2.1 x 9.5 cm.
127	2.2 x 11.0 cm.
128	2.2 x 11.0 cm.
129	2.2 x 13.1 cm.
130	2.2 x 13.1 cm.
131	2.2 x 13.1 cm.
132	2.2 x 13.1 cm.
133	2.2 x 13.1 cm.
134	2.2 x 13.1 cm.
135	2.3 x 13.1 cm.
136	2.3 x 13.1 cm.
137	2.5 x 13.1 cm.
138	2.5 x 13.1 cm.
139	2.6 x 13.2 cm.
140	2.6 x 13.2 cm.
141	2.5 x 13.2 cm.
142	2.5 x 13.2 cm.
143	21.3 x 13.2 cm.
144	21.3 x 13.2 cm.

145	21.3 x 13.2 cm.
146	21.3 x 13.2 cm.
147	21.3 x 13.2 cm.
148	21.3 x 13.2 cm.
149	21.3 x 13.2 cm.
150	21.3 x 13.2 cm.
151	21.3 x 13.2 cm.
152	21.3 x 13.2 cm.
153	21.3 x 13.2 cm.
154	21.3 x 13.2 cm.
155	21.3 x 13.2 cm.
156	21.3 x 13.2 cm.
157	21.3 x 13.2 cm.
158	21.3 x 13.2 cm.
159	21.3 x 13.2 cm.
160	21.3 x 13.2 cm.
161	21.3 x 13.2 cm.
162	21.2 x 13.2 cm.
163	21.3 x 13.2 cm.
164	21.3 x 13.2 cm.
165	21.3 x 13.2 cm.
166	21.3 x 13.2 cm.
167	21.3 x 13.2 cm.
168	21.3 x 13.2 cm.
169	0.9 x 13.1 cm.
170	0.9 x 13.1 cm.
171	4.5 x 13.2 cm.
172	4.5 x 13.2 cm.
173	6.3 x 13.2 cm.
174	6.3 x 13.2 cm.
175	6.3 x 13.2 cm.
176	6.3 x 13.2 cm.
177	4.3 x 13.2 cm.
178	4.3 x 13.2 cm.
179	5.0 x 13.2 cm.
180	5.0 x 13.2 cm.
181	3.0 x 13.2 cm.
182	3.0 x 13.2 cm.
183	3.0 x 13.2 cm.
184	3.0 x 13.2 cm.
185	2.0 x 8.3 cm.
186	2.0 x 8.3 cm.
187	1.8 x 8.2 cm.
188	1.8 x 8.2 cm.
189	1.7 x 6.4 cm.
190	1.7 x 6.4 cm.
191	1.5 x 5.5 cm.
192	1.5 x 5.5 cm.

Abstract of Draft Usage

***Blue*-deleted material appears in**

I.2§ 1.*1: Fair copy (ink, but with pencil revisions); August-September 1923-October 1923).
II.3§7.*2: Fair copy (ink) of 'Roderick O'Conor', July 1923.
II.4§2.0/3A.*1: First draft (pencil); sent to Harriet Shaw Weaver on 5 October 1923.
IV§2.*2: Fair copy (ink) of 'St Kevin'; July 1923.
IV§2.*3: Fair copy (ink) of 'St Kevin'; July 1923.

***Brown*-deleted material**

These units are too fragmentary to read in the notebook as it stands today: they were very probably transferred to the early drafts of 'Roderick O'Connor', 'Tristan' and 'Kevin'.

***Green*-deleted material appears in**

I.8§1.5': Duplicate (carbon) of typescript separately revised; July 1925. (One item.)
III§4.*2: Fair copy (ink); probably March-April 1926.

***Orange*-deleted material appears in**

I.1§1.*2/2.*2: Fair copy (ink), dated by Joyce 29 November 1926, but some insertions made at a later date).
I.6§1.4': Galley proofs (First set: comprising *FW* 126-150.14, 168.13-14) for *transition* 6; keyed to be followed by §2.2; probably early August 1927.

***Red*-deleted material appears in**

I.1§2B.*1: Second draft (pencil) in the red notebook, including the first available draft of *FW* 23.16-29; November 1926.
I.2§2.*0: First draft (pencil and ink) of *FW* 34.34-44.08, written at the beginning of a large red-backed notebook; October 1923.
I.2§2.*1: Fair copy (pencil), in the large red-backed notebook; October 1923. (One item.)
I.2§2.2/3.2 Fair copy (ink), written in two parts but later combined by Joyce; probably November-December 1923.
I.3§1.*0: First draft (pencil) of *FW* 48-50.32, 57.16-61.27, written in a large red-backed notebook; November 1923. (One item.)
I.3§1.*1: Second draft (pencil) of *FW* 48-50.32, 57.16-61.27, written in a large red-backed notebook; November 1923. (One item.)
I.3§1.*2/2.*2/3.*2: Fair copy (ink); November-December 1923.
I.3§1.*4/2.*4/3.*4: Fair copy (ink); March 1927.
I.3§2.*1: Second draft (pencil), in the same notebook; November 1923.
I.4§1A.*1: Fair copy (pencil), November-December 1923.
I.4§IA.*2: Fair copy (ink), uniform with and following on the same page the end of I.3§3.*2; December 1923-January 1924.
I.4§2.*0: First draft (pencil) of *FW* 096.26-101.25, in the large red-backed notebook; November-December 1923. (One item.)
I.4§2.*1: Fair copy (pencil), including an extension to *FW* 102.17, in the same notebook; December 1923-January 1924.
I.5§1.*0: First draft (pencil) of *FW* 104-112.02, written in a large red-backed notebook; December 1923.
I.5§1.*1: Second draft (pencil) in the red-backed notebook; December 1923.
I.5§2.*0: First draft (pencil) of 'The Revered Letter', in the red-backed notebook; December 1923.
I.5§2.*1: Second draft (pencil) in the same notebook, following immediately on the same page the end of I.4§2.*1; December 1923.
I.5§4.*0: First draft (pencil) in the red-backed notebook; probably December 1923-January 1924.
I.7§1.*0: First draft (pencil) in a large red-backed notebook; January 1924.
I.7§1.*1: Second draft (pencil) in the same notebook; January 1924.
I.7§1.3/2.3: First typescript, probably February 1924, but revised April-May 1925.
I.8§1A.*1/lB.*1: Second draft (pencil) including the first available draft of *FW* 208.27-216; February 1924.
II.4§1.*1: Second fair copy of 'Tristan and Isolde' (ink); August 1923.
II.4§2.*0/3A.*1: First draft (pencil); sent to Harriet Shaw Weaver on 5 October 1923.
III§1A.*2/1D.*2//2A.*2/2C.*2: Fair copy (pencil); May 1924.
III§3B.*2: Third draft (pencil) of 'Haveth Childers Everywhere'; December 1924.
III§4.*2: Fair copy (ink); probably March-April 1926. Red crayon probably used erroneously here for green.
IV§2.*3: Fair copy (ink) of 'St Kevin'; July 1923.

Transcription of Notebook VI.B.25

Only those pages, or page fragments, containing sufficient markings to make transcription possible have been reproduced.

VI.B.25.001-7 [not in *JJA*] [blank]

VI.B.25.008 [not in *JJA*]

(a) *[??]*

VI.B.25.009 [001 in *JJA*]

VI.B.25.009 [001 in *JJA*]

(a) **Irish speak */low/***

VI.A.0031 ('An Encounter'): 'I speak low'.

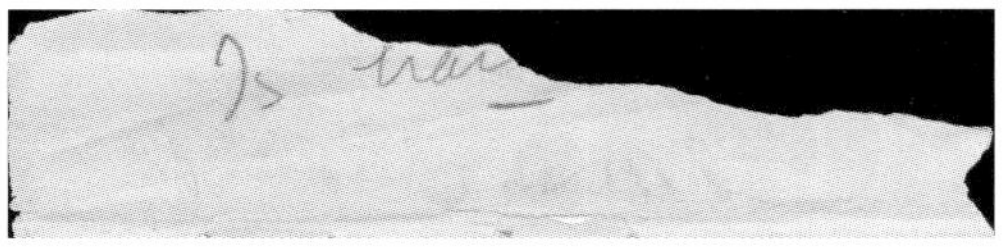

VI.B.25.010 [002 in *JJA*]

VI.B.25.010 [002 in *JJA*]

(a) **Is */har/***

VI.B.25.011 [003 in *JJA*]

VI.B.25.011 [003 in *JJA*]

(a) **Chapelizod ~~drill~~ band**

(b) *[??]*

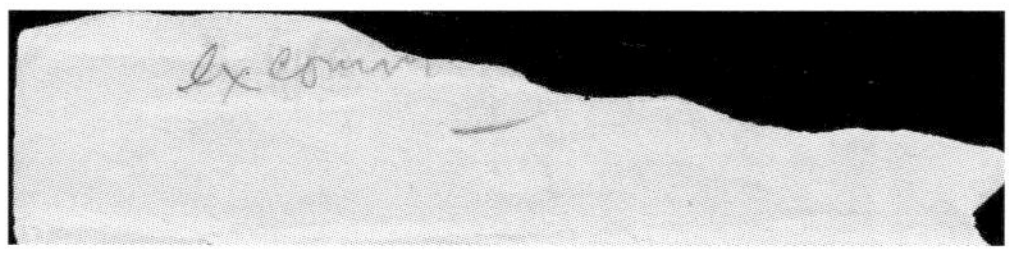

VI.B.25.012 [004 in *JJA*]

VI.B.25.012 [004 in *JJA*]

(a) **excomm*[??]***

VI.B.25.013 [005 in *JJA*]

VI.B.25.013 [005 in *JJA*]

(a) **S Kevin's Chapel — pro / Cathe/dral Dublin/**

Note: The Roman Catholic Pro-Cathedral is in Marlborough Street, Dublin (see *FW* 569.14). Dermod McCarthy, in his booklet *Saint Mary's Pro-Cathedral* (Dublin: Eason & Son Ltd., 1988), pp. 20-2, gives the following account of its designation: 'Visitors to the church frequently ask why it is called a Pro-Cathedral. It came to be known as such in the 1880s and it was Dr Walsh who confirmed the use of that title. St. Lawrence O'Toole, second Archbishop of Dublin, rebuilt and enlarged Christ Church and it was constituted by the Pope at the time as the Cathedral of the Holy Trinity. In the seven centuries that have elapsed since then no successor of St. Lawrence has asked for that decision to be revoked. Until that happens, St. Mary's will continue as the mother church, but without the full title of 'cathedral' of Dublin.'

The original St Kevin's Chapel no longer exists. It was situated in the northern flank but incorporated into the main body of the building in the late 1920s, when a new building was erected on the same side to replace it. This is known as St Kevin's Oratory.

VI.A.0032 ('An Encounter'): 'Kevin's chapel procathedral'.

VI.B.25.014 [006 in *JJA*]

VI.B.25.014 [006 in *JJA*]

(a) **num*[??]***

(b) ***/aunt ??/***

VI.B.25.015 [007 in *JJA*]

(a) **far other**

(b) ***/hi??/***

VI.B.25.015 [007 in *JJA*]

VI.B.25.016 [008 in *JJA*]

(a) *[??]*

(b) ***/mare in ??/***

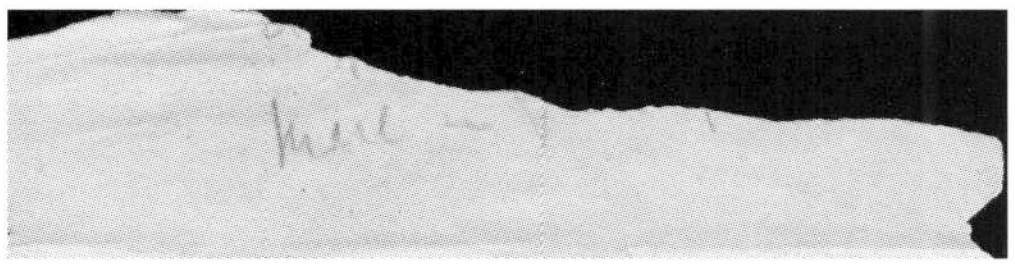

VI.B.25.016 [008 in *JJA*]

VI.B.25.017 [009 in *JJA*]

(a) [r]**culprit**

MS 47471a-36, MT: O phenix culprit! | *JJA* 44:099 | Nov 1926 | I.1§2B.*1 | *FW* 023.16

(b) *[??]*

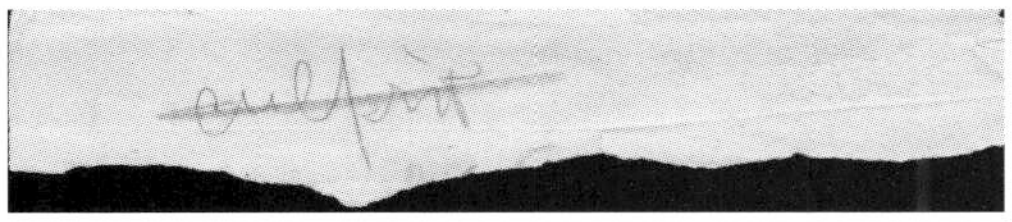

VI.B.25.017 [009 in *JJA*]

VI.B.25.018 [010 in *JJA*]

(a) *[??]*

(b) **biz v pleas*/ure/***

MS 47471b-40, MT: he always sits forenenst me ^+, poor ass,+^ to make our conversation about business & pleasure | Dec 1923 | I.5§2.*1 | 'The Revered Letter' [→] MS 47488-124, MT: polite conversation with a huntered per scent human over ^+the+^ natural bestness of pleisure | *JJA* 63:193 | IV§4.*0 | Sep-Oct 1938 [*FW* 618.36-619.01]

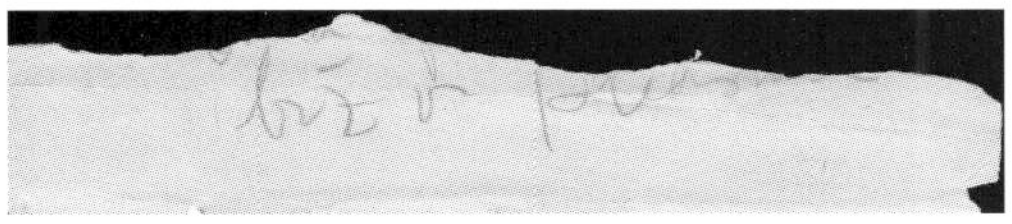

VI.B.25.018 [010 in *JJA*]

VI.B.25.019 [011 in *JJA*]

(a) **Irish tricolour at / */foretruck/***

Note: Foretruck. The small cap at the head of the foremast of a ship, with holes for the halliard.

VI.B.25.019 [011 in *JJA*]

VI.B.25.020 [012 in *JJA*]

(a) *[??]*

VI.B.25.021 [013 in *JJA*]

(a) [r]**florist**

MS 47471b-52v, MT: ~~walking~~ ^+taking a short cut+^ [...] into a ^+Patatapapaveri's+^ fruiterer & florist | *JJA* 47:336 | Jan 1924 | I.7§1.*0 | *FW* 172.02

VI.B.25.021 [013 in *JJA*]

VI.B.25.022 [014 in *JJA*] [blank]

VI.B.25.023 [015 in *JJA*]

VI.B.25.023 [015 in *JJA*]

(a) **/Gin/gerbread built / /??/ Dominick**

Freeman's Journal 25 June 1923-8/7: [By the Way] The City "State Coach." A reference was made in a recent speech to the old-time civic processions in Dublin / The coach was in fact built by John Whitton, coachbuilder, in Dominick street, in the year 1790 [...] In 1807 an iconoclastic Alderman had the temerity to propose that the vehicle (which had come to be known colloquially as the "Gingerbread") should be sold.

Note: See VI.B.28.196 and VI.C.10.054: 'Whitton / John / mayor coach', which formed the basis for *FW* 359.23-4. 'Whiston' here is a typist's error; the reference in *Annotations* (1991) should be corrected.

VI.A.0034 ('An Encounter'): 'John Whislton built / gingerbread'.

VI.B.25.024 [016 in *JJA*] [blank]

VI.B.25.025 [017 in *JJA*]

VI.B.25.025 [017 in *JJA*]

(a) **start of Chapel tram**

Note: Presumably the Lucan tram, which served Chapelizod. This started in Conyngham road (*FW* 576.28). See also VI.B.3.002(a).

(b) **/Trist/ fiddle /??/**

VI.B.25.026 [018 in *JJA*] [blank]

VI.B.25.027 [019 in *JJA*]

VI.B.25.027 [019 in *JJA*]

(a) **no more tay for / /??/ th/??/**

VI.A.0034 ('An Encounter'): 'no more / tay for sugar the cosey'.

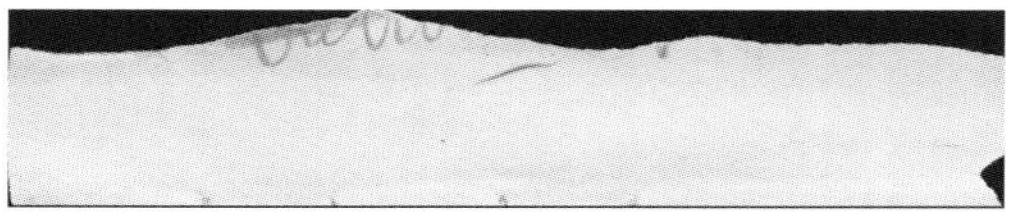

VI.B.25.028 [020 in *JJA*]

VI.B.25.028 [020 in *JJA*]

(a) **[r]/bath ??/**

?VI.A.0040 ('An Encounter'): 'bath copper'.

VI.B.25.029 [021 in *JJA*]

VI.B.25.029 [021 in *JJA*]

(a) **Mrs /.../**

(b) **/??/**

VI.B.25.030 [022 in *JJA*]

VI.B.25.030 [022 in *JJA*]

(a) **/iron cross/**

(b) **drift line**

Guide to Bognor 12: A drift line from the west side of the Pier should be used when the tide is just touching the beach

VI.B.25.031 [023 in *JJA*]

VI.B.25.031 [023 in *JJA*]

(a) [b]**paternoster (bait)**

*Guide to Bognor*12: Fishing with 'Paternoster' is recommended from the Pier, as various depths of the bait will suit the habits of different fish.

Note: Paternoster-line. A fishing line with hooks attached at intervals; so called because of the resulting resemblance to rosary beads. See also VI.B.2.053(j) 'bait the trout / (line with 40 hooks)'. Although this VI.B.2 entry was not transferred it forms part of a short fishing index, which was used for the next draft (I.2§1.*2) of *FW* 031.

MS 47472-98, ILS: ~~inquiring~~ ^+~~??~~ ^+asking to be put wise+^+^ whether ~~he had not been engaged in~~ ^+ ~~whitebait~~ ^+paternoster+^ were not now more fancied ^+bait+^ for+^ lobster trapping | *JJA* 45:004 | Aug-Sep 1923 | I.2§1.*1 | *FW* 031.07

(b) *[??]*

VI.B.25.032 [024 in *JJA*]

(a) [o]*[??]*

VI.B.25.033 [025 in *JJA*]

VI.B.25.033 [025 in *JJA*]

(a) [b]**Vigilance Committee**

Note: 'The Irish Vigilance Association' was founded in 1911, under the auspices of the Dominicans. Its primary purpose was to protect Irish Catholics from the excesses of the English popular press. Volunteers were sought and a number of Vigilance Committees were set up in various parts of the country. See letter dated 11 February 1922, in *James Joyce's Letters to Sylvia Beach*.

MS 47472-98v, ILA: ^+at the instance of kind ^+Watch Warriors+^ vigilance committee+^ | *JJA* 45:007 | Aug-Sep 1923 | I.2§1.*1 | *FW* 034.04

VI.B.25.034 [026 in *JJA*]

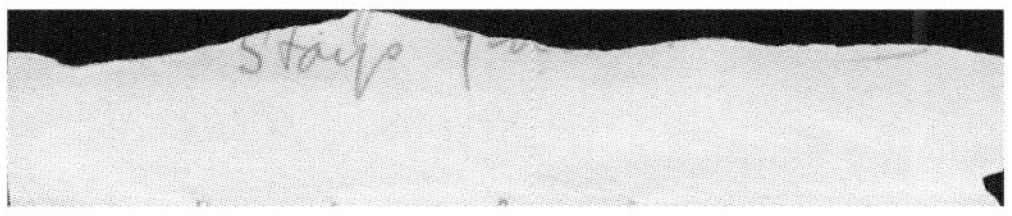

VI.B.25.034 [026 in *JJA*]

(a) *[??]*

(b) **stays y*[*oung*]***

VI.B.25.035 [027 in *JJA*]

VI.B.25.035 [027 in *JJA*]

(a) **mantrap with crocodile / *[??]* (abol. 1827)**

Note: Since 1827 mantraps have been illegal in England (see 11th *EB* 'Man-Traps' 607b). The 'crocodile' (as in 'crocodile-clip') presumably refers to part of the mechanism, such as the jaws of the trap.

VI.B.25.036 [028 in *JJA*]

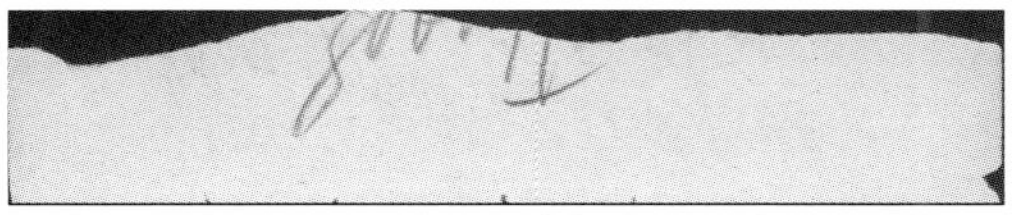

VI.B.25.036 [028 in *JJA*]

(a) **go*[*o??*]***

VI.B.25.037 [029 in *JJA*]

VI.B.25.037 [029 in *JJA*]

(a) **/Schein ingest rumpet/**

(b) *[??]*

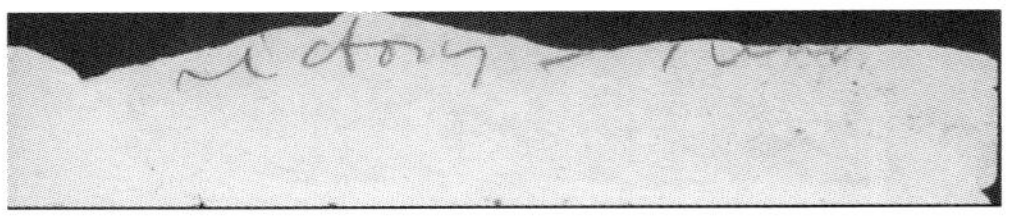

VI.B.25.038 [030 in *JJA*]

VI.B.25.038 [030 in *JJA*]

(a) **victory -** *[??]*

VI.B.25.039 [031 in *JJA*]

(a) *[??]*

VI.B.25.040-54 [not in *JJA*] [blank]

Note: Thirty-three leaves (sixty-six pages) have been torn from the notebook at this point.

VI.B.25.055 [not in *JJA*]

(a) *[??]*

VI.B.25.056 [not in *JJA*] [blank]

VI.B.25.057 [not in *JJA*]

(a) *[??]*

VI.B.25.058-104 [not in *JJA*] [blank]

Note: This represents the centre of the original notebook. See colour reproduction at the end of this volume.

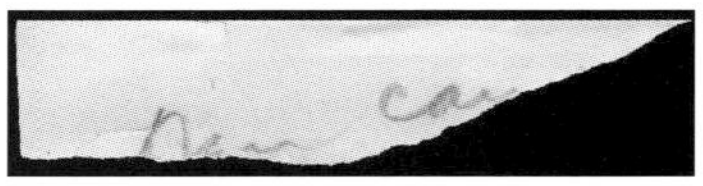

VI.B.25.105 [031 in *JJA*]

VI.B25.105 [031 in *JJA*]

(a) **/grain car/** *[??]*

VI.B.25.106 [032 in *JJA*] [blank]

Note: The *JJA* reproduction shows fragment of text from 038 [032 in *JJA*] behind this page.

VI.B.25.107 [033 in *JJA*]

VI.B.25.107 [033 in *JJA*]

(a) **Sinn Fa/ne/**

Note: Sinn Féin. The radical nationalist party founded by Arthur Griffith and Bulmer Hobson in 1905. The name derives from a nationalist slogan, commonly translated as 'ourselves alone', which predates the party. Here it appears to be the basis of a pun, 'sin' + 'fane' (a temple).

(b) *[??]*

VI.B.25.108 [034 in *JJA*]

(a) ^{br}*/*sod*?/*

VI.B.25.108 [034 in *JJA*]

VI.B.25.109 [035 in *JJA*]

(a) ^{r}*/*lead us not*/*

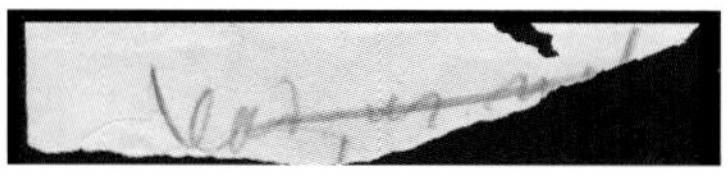

VI.B.25.109 [035 in *JJA*]

VI.B.25.108 and VI.B.25.109 are reproduced in colour at the end of this volume

VI.B.25.110 [036 in *JJA*] [blank]

VI.B.25.111 [037 in *JJA*]

(a) *[??]*

VI.B.25.112 [038 in *JJA*]

(a) *[??]*

VI.B.25.113 [039 in *JJA*]

(a) the *[??]*

VI.B.25.113 [039 in *JJA*]

VI.B.25.114 [040 in *JJA*]

(a) *[??]*

VI.B.25.115 [041 in *JJA*]

(a) ^{br}like

Not found in MS/*FW*

VI.B.25.115 [041 in *JJA*]

VI.B.25.116 [042 in *JJA*] [blank]

VI.B.25.117 [043 in *JJA*]

(a) *[??]*

VI.B.25.118 [044 in *JJA*]

(a) *[*co*?]*

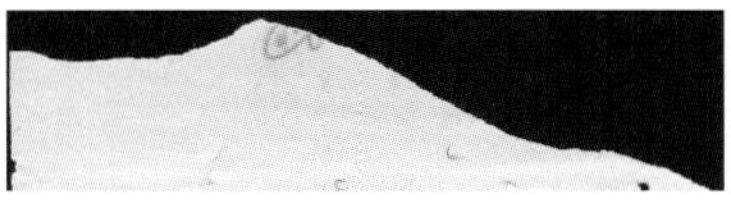

VI.B.25.118 [044 in *JJA*]

VI.B.25.119 [045 in *JJA*]

VI.B.25.119 [045 in *JJA*]

(a) **/G/reat** */??/*

VI.B.25.120 [046 in *JJA*]

VI.B.25.120 [046 in *JJA*]

(a) ^{b}**/g***?/*

VI.B.25.120 is reproduced in colour at the end of this volume

VI.B.25.121 [047 in *JJA*]

(a) ^{r}*/??/*

VI.B.25.122 [048 in *JJA*]

(a) */??/*

VI.B.25.123 [049 in *JJA*]

VI.B.25.123 [049 in *JJA*]

(a) */??/* **S/oul/** */??/*

VI.B.25.124 [050 in *JJA*]

VI.B.25.124 [050 in *JJA*]

(a) **an** */??/*

VI.B.25.125 [051 in *JJA*]

(a) */??/*

VI.B.25.126 [052 in *JJA*]

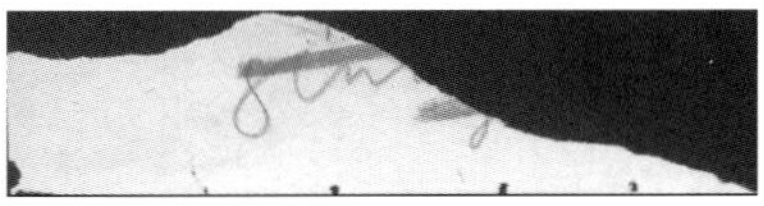

VI.B.25.126 [052 in *JJA*]

(a) ^{r}**sin/ning society/**

MS 47471b-2v, LMA: fashionable vice preacher to whom ^+sinning+^ society ~~ladies~~ +^beauties+^ […] became so enthusiasticaly attached | *JJA* 45:137 | Nov 1923 | I.3§1.*0 | *FW* 050.23

VI.B.25.126 is reproduced in colour at the end of this volume

VI.B.25.127 [053 in *JJA*]

(a) */??/*

VI.B.25.128 [054 in *JJA*]

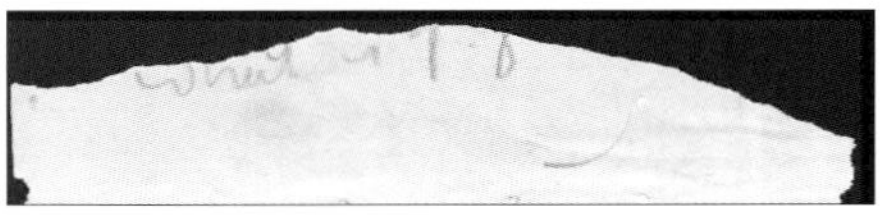

VI.B.25.128 [054 in *JJA*]

(a) **what is** */??/*

VI.B.25.129 [055 in *JJA*]

VI.B.25.129 [055 in *JJA*]

(a) [r]**perfectly proud of** ***[??]***

MS 47471b-33, MT: I am perfectly proud of Mr Earwicker | *JJA* 46:259 | Dec 1923 | I.5§2.*0 | 'The Revered Letter' *FDV* 082.38

(b) **d***[?]*

VI.B.25.130 [056 in *JJA*] [blank]

VI.B.25.131 [057 in *JJA*]

VI.B.25.131 [057 in *JJA*]

(a) ***/??*** **of/ Earw/icker/**

VI.B.25.132 [058 in *JJA*]

(a) ***[??]***

VI.B.25.133 [059 in *JJA*]

VI.B.25.133 [059 in *JJA*]

(a) **/croo/ked stick & grey goose** ***[??]***

Note: See the *Oxford Dictionary of English Proverbs*, 'England were but a fling, save for the crooked stick and the greygoose wing.' A note explains this as a reference to archery. 'Fling' is not glossed here, but it is defined by the *OED* as 'A thing of no importance'. The VI.A note, transcribed below, has lost the rhyme and with it much of the proverbial impact.

VI.A.0044 ('Araby'): 'crooked stick & grey goose quill'

VI.B.25.134 [060 in *JJA*]

(a) ***[??]***

VI.B.25.135 [061 in *JJA*]

(a) [r]***[??]***

VI.B.25.136 [062 in *JJA*]

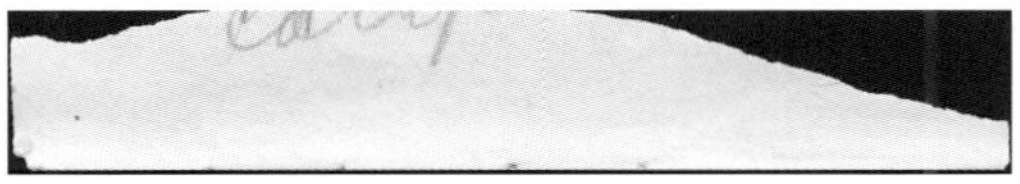

VI.B.25.136 [062 in *JJA*]

(a) **cara/pace/**

VI.B.25.137 [063 in *JJA*]

VI.B.25.137 [063 in *JJA*]

(a) **/S*??*/ic Review**

Note: See reproduction. The title as transcribed appears to begin with, or contain an uppercase 's'. One possibility, on circumstantial grounds, is the *Asiatic Review*: Vol XIX, No. 59 appeared in July 1923 and included a series of articles on various aspects of India.

VI.B.25.138 [064 in *JJA*] [blank]

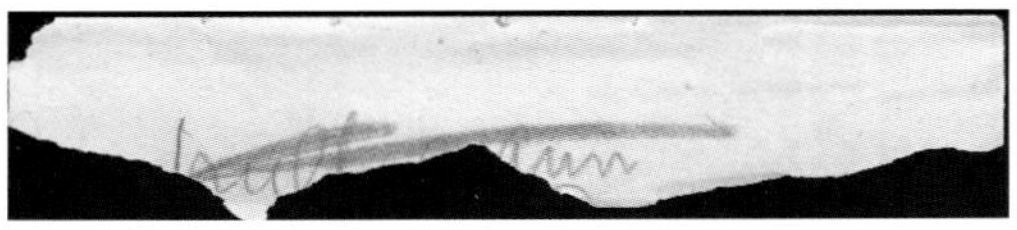

VI.B.25.139 [055 in *JJA*]

VI.B.25.139 [065 in *JJA*]

(a) **ʳpull a gun**

MS 47471b-33, MT: If any […] thick goes to pull a gun on me | *JJA* 46:259 | Dec 1923 | I.5§2.*0 |'The Revered Letter' *FDV* 082.35

VI.B.25.140 [066 in *JJA*] [blank]

VI.B.25.141 [067 in *JJA*]

VI.B.25.141 [067 in *JJA*]

(a) **Tim Healy got / *[??]*any**

Note: Timothy Healy (1855-1931). At the time of this entry he was Ireland's first Governor-General.

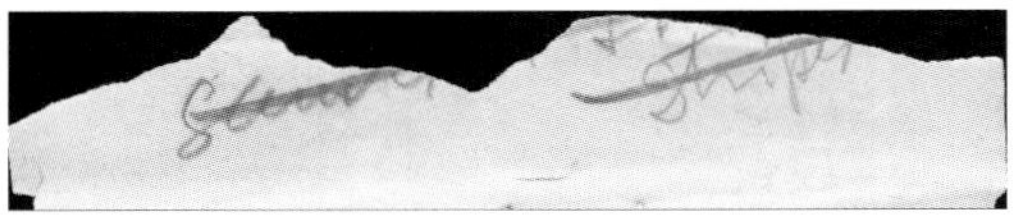

VI.B.25.142 [068 in *JJA*]

VI.B.25.142 [068 in *JJA*]

(a) **ʳsaints *[??]* / — stripes**

Note: Proverbs 17:10: 'More profitable to saints, than stripes to a fool'.

MS 47471b-88, MT: ~~a~~ ^+the+^ flag of the saints & stripes for Kevineen O'Dea | *JJA* 48:033 | Feb 1924 | I.8§1A.*1/1B.*1 | *FW* 210.13

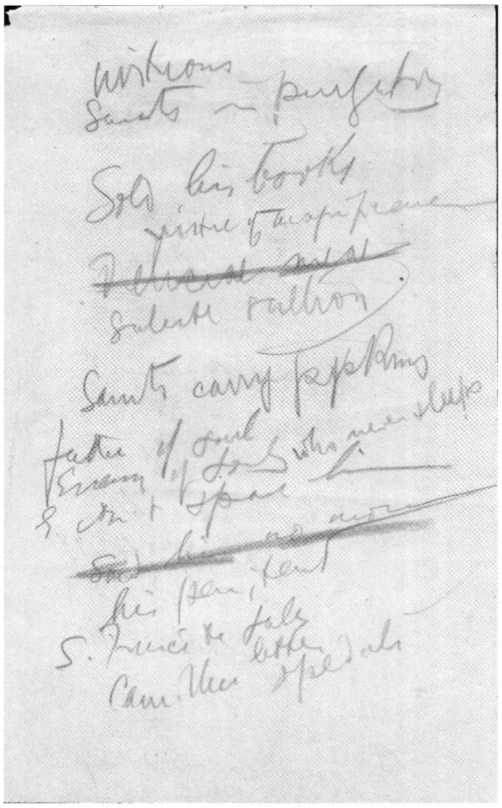

VI.B.25.143 [069 in *JJA*]

VI.B.25.143 [069 in *JJA*]

(a) **virtuous / souls in purgatory**

(b) **Sold his books**

(c) **virtue of magnificence**

(d) **ʳDeliciae meae**

Note: L. *Deliciae meae*. My delights; my darling. In its various meanings it is common in classical Latin literature. Here its source is almost certainly scriptural or patristic. See Vulgate, *Proverbs* 8: 30-1: *cum eo eram […] ludens in orbe terrarum et deliciæ meæ esse cum filiis hominum.* [King James, *Proverbs* 8:30-1: Then I was by him […] Rejoicing in the habitable part of his earth; and my delights were with the sons of men.]

Not located in MS/*FW*

(e) **salute scullion**

(f) **Saints carry pipkins**

Note: Pipkin. A small earthenware pot.

(g) **father of soul**

(h) **Enemy of souls / ^+who never sleeps+^**

(i) **G. cdn't spare him**

(j) **ʳsaw him no more**

MS 47472-120, LMA: ^+after which he and Pump court saw each other no more for it seems that on the other side of the water he perished.+^ | *JJA* 45:171 | Nov-Dec 1923 | I.3§1.*2/2.*2/3.*2 | *FW* 049.11

(k) **his penitent**

(l) **S. Francis de Sales**

Note: St Francis de Sales (1622-55). French bishop and writer. Indefatigable preacher against Calvinism and author of the widely translated *Introduction à la vie dévote*.

(m) **letter**

(n) **Camillus spedali**

Note: It. *Spedali*. Hospitals. Saint Camillus de Lellis (1550-1614) was a nurse and the founder of the Fathers of a Good Death, devoted to the care of the sick.

VI.B.25.144 [070 in *JJA*]

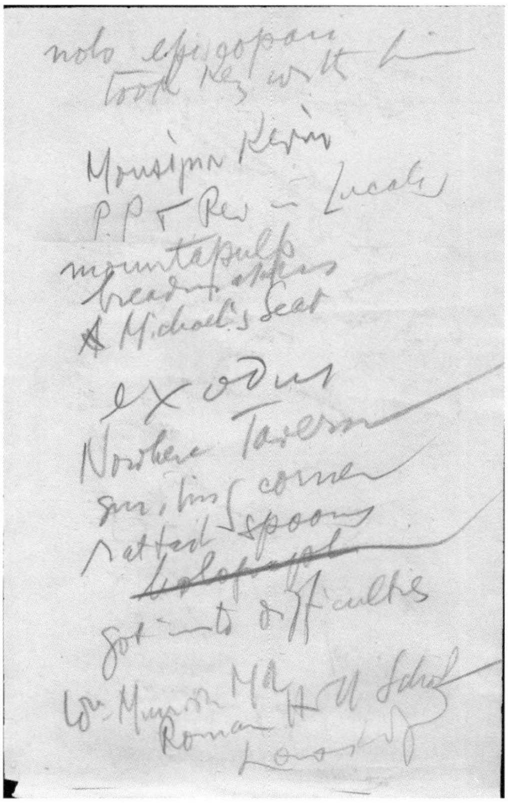

VI.B.25.144 [070 in *JJA*]

(a) **nolo episcopari**

Note: L. *Nolo episcopari*. I am unwilling to accept the office of bishop. See entry under this heading in Brewer's *Dictionary of Phrase and Fable*, which dismisses as a popular fallacy the notion that this is a phrase used by bishops at their consecration.

(b) **took key with him**

(c) **Monsignor Kevin**

VI.A.0045 ('Araby'): 'Mgr Kevin'

(d) **P.P. & Rev in Lucali/zod/**

Note: See reproduction. If this reading is correct, the word has been abbreviated. Lucalizod is a portmanteau (apparently Joyce's), composed of Lucan and Chapelizod. It is first noted at VI.B.10.033(f) and makes a number of appearances in Book I of the *Wake*.

(e) **mountapulp**

(f) **breadmakers**

(g) **~~A~~ Michael's Seat**

(h) **exodus**

(i) **Nowhere Tavern**

(j) **smiling corner**

(k) **rattail spoons**

Note: Rat-tail (or rat-tailed) spoon. A spoon having a prolongation of the handle along the back of the bowl, thought to resemble a rat's tail.

(l) **[b]holograph**

MS 47472-98, ILS: all ~~documents~~ ^+holographs+^ initialled by Haromphrey bear the sigla H.C.E | *JJA* 45:005 | Aug-Sep 1923 | I.2§1.*1 | *FW* 032.13

(m) **got into difficulties**

(n) **W$^{\underline{m}}$ M/unish/ M of / Roman Hill School / Lowesoft**

Note: There is still a Roman Hill School in Lowestoft, East Suffolk. It takes its name from the Roman Hill area in west Lowestoft, a site where a number of Roman coins were found. There is no record there of anyone with a name similar to 'Munish'.

M. Here probably an abbreviation of 'master'.

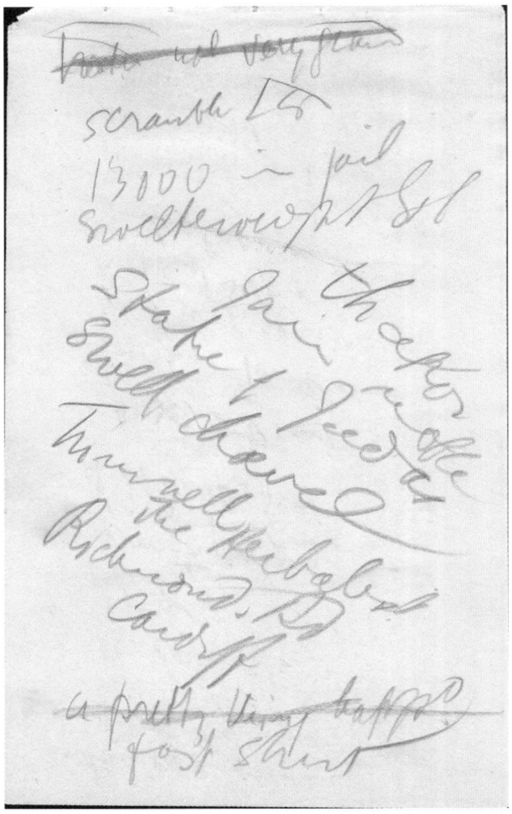

VI.B.25.145 [071 in *JJA*]

VI.B.25.145 [071 in *JJA*]

(a) **[r]treated not very grand**

MS 47471b-33, MT: So much for the ~~lies~~ ^+sneakery+^ that I was treated not very grand by thicks | *JJA* 46:259 | Dec 1923 | I.5§2.*0 | 'The Revered Letter' *FDV* 082.33 [→] MS 47488-124, MT: That I was ^+we were+^ treated not very grand when the police and everybody is all bowing to us | *JJA* 63:193 | IV§4.*0 | Sep-Oct 1938 | *FW* 618.20

(b) **scramble Lsd**

(c) **13000 in jail**

(d) **swelterweight /Gvt/**

Note: Swelterweight. In boxing 'welter weight' is a grade between light-weight and middle-weight. The term is also used for a heavy-weight horseman. Here it has been combined with 'swelter' to form a portmanteau.

(e) **that for / Jain noble**

Note: Jain. A member of the Jainist sect. Jainism, an East Indian ascetic sect bearing some resemblance to Buddhism, was founded around the sixth century B.C. Its principal doctrine is that of noninjury of living creatures.

(f) **statue of Judas**

?Daily Mail 19 July 1923-13/2: [Statue to Judas Iscariot / Red's Blasphemous Farce] The well-known Danish writer [...] M. Halling-Koehler, who has been travelling in Russia, has given a description of a scene which he witnessed there [...] It was M. Halling-Koehler's lot to travel to the small town of Sviashsk, near Kazan, on the occasion of the unveiling there of a statue to Judas Iscariot. [...] Before the great draped statue stood a red-bearded Soviet leader, who delivered the inauguratory speech. He declared that the committee had hesitated between three candidates to statuehood—Lucifer, Cain, and Judas Iscariot.

(g) **sweet chervil**

Note: Sweet chervil. *Myrrhis odorata*. A garden herb, also known as 'sweet Cicely'.

(h) **Trimnell / The Herbalist / Richmond Rd / Cardiff**

Note: See also VI.A.461 and VI.B.11.056(d). The following advertisement appeared regularly in *the Irish Homestead* and in its successor, (from 1922) the *Irish Statesman*, from September 15th 1923: '64-Page Book about Herbs and how to use them, 2d. Send for one. Trimnel, The Herbalist, Richmond Road, Cardiff'.

(i) **[r]a pretty thing happened**

MS 47481-95v, LMA: Milky way strew dim light! / ^+Here a pretty thing happened.+^ When ~~he~~ ^+[...]+^ had ^+jessaminely+^ shut his duckhouse | *JJA* 56:011 | Aug 1923 | II.4§1.*1 | *FW* 395.26

(j) **fast shirt**

VI.B.25.146 [072 in *JJA*]

(a) **die on bare ground**

(b) **Actum est de / Hibernia**

Note: L. *Actum est de Hibernia*. Ireland is done for.

(c) **ghost**

(d) **to take in** ***[??]***

(e) **process of fame / of sanctity**

Note: One of the earliest stages in canonization is the preparation of the inquiries (*processus*) about the suitability of the candidate. These include compilation of an account of the reputation for sanctity (super fama). See *CE* 'Beatification', 367c, 368a.

(f) ***[Ocru of Kraz]*** **/ 1 Virtues / 2 miracles**

Note: Both virtues and miracles are prerequisites for sainthood.

(g) **safe to proceed**

(h) **philautia**

Note: Philautia. Self-love; selfishness.

(i) **'*[How]* grateful should / be' For he it was / that said if God said / ⌈may I say it — / offence. I rarely / *[hear]* service / in one man**

MS 47482b-32v, LPA: ^+Thy now paling lamp we may perchance ne'er see again. Ah, if it could ^+only+^ speak how it ~~could~~ ^+would+^ splutter~~!~~ ^+out+^ praises be to thee. For you had - may I say it? - a glow of zeal of service such as ~~I have rarely~~ ^+rarely, if ever, have I seen+^ seen in any man's bosom.+^ | *JJA* 57:066 | May 1924 | III§1A.*2/1D.*2//2A.*2/2C.*2 | *FW* 472.25

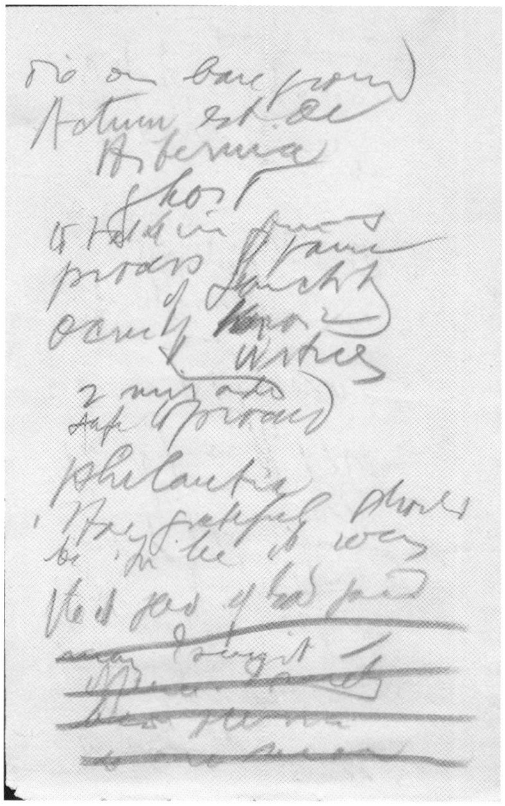

VI.B.25.146 [072 in *JJA*]

VI.B.25.147 [073 in *JJA*]

(a) **Is changes skirt / walking**

(b) **presented bell chimes**

(c) **Book of Common / Prayer / (Mitford) 5/-**

(d) **The Man of Promise / (Moses)**

?Daily News 3 July 1923-7/3: [Review] "The Man of Promise: Lord Roseberry" by E.T. Raymond, T. Fisher Unwin. 10*s*.

(e) **Sponsa Dei / (Patmore) >**

(f) **Hopkins said—that's telling secrets**

Quarterly Review July 1923, 132: [Coventry Patmore by John Freeman] In one lost essay, the fruit of ten years meditation, he pursued the familiar sex symbol, and Mr. Gosse has told us of the lamentable destruction of 'Sponsa Dei,' the entire manuscript being burned as a result of the author's conversation with Father Gerard Hopkins; for Hopkins, himself a poet of incalculable because unintelligible genius, had said, 'That's telling secrets,' when he read the essay and saw how it developed Patmore's central theme. Ready as the author was to fulfil the highest office of a poet by telling secrets that were lawful, the peril of telling secrets that his church might think it unlawful to tell was too great.

(g) **bid up against**

(h) **dog piece of raw / *[catmeat]***

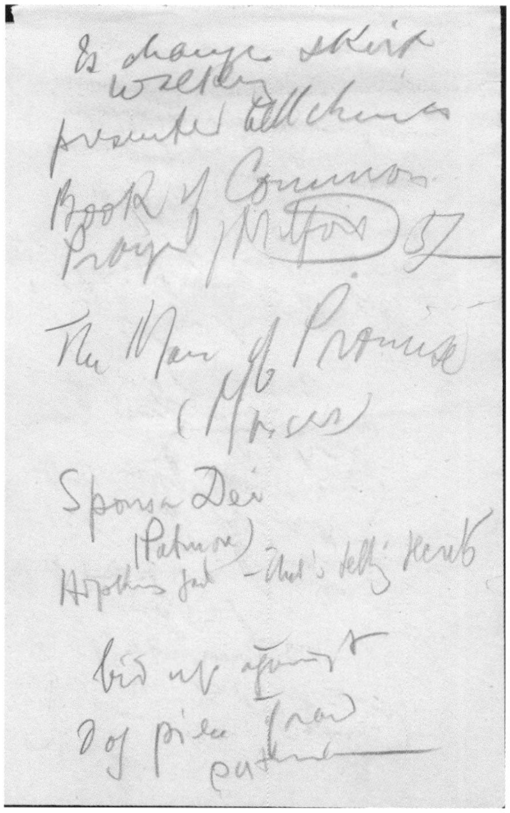

VI.B.25.147 [073 in *JJA*]

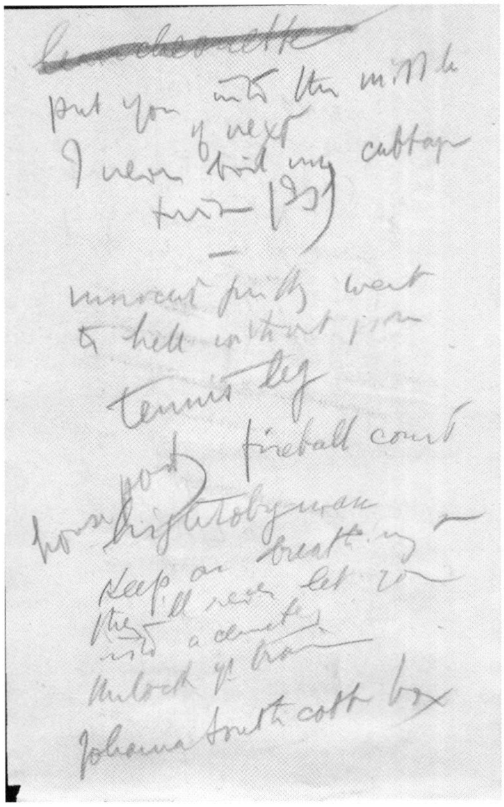

VI.B.25.148 [074 in *JJA*]

VI.B.25.148 and VI.B.25.149 are reproduced in colour at the end of this volume

VI.B.25.148 [074 in *JJA*]

(a) **^{r}luncheonette**

Note: Luncheonette. A snack bar serving light lunches. Earliest *OED* citation 1924.
MS 47472-131, ILA: without even a lunch ^+luncheonette+^ interval. | *JJA* 45:182 | Nov-Dec 1923 | I.3§1.*2/2.*2/<u>3.*2</u> | *FW* 070.33-4

(b) **put you into the middle / of next**

(c) **I never boil my cabbage / twice (Is)**

(d) **innocent guilty went / to hell without sin**

(e) **tennis leg**

(f) **fireball courts**

(g) **housepost**

(h) **hightobyman**

Note: 'Toby' is Shelta for 'road', hence 'hightobyman' is a partial translation of 'highwayman'. See entry in Eric Partridge's *Dictionary of the Underworld.*

(i) **Keep on breathing & / they'll never let you / into a cemetery**

(j) **Unlock y^r brain**

(k) **Johanna Southcott box**

Evening Standard 27 July 1923-4/3: [A Londoner's Diary] Johanna Southcott's Box. / I have discovered that there is a box containing the writings of Johanna Southcott in existence, and that it has been opened recently. / It is not the box concerning which there has been so much controversy but the contents are probably similar. This box is now in the basement of the Church House at Westminster.
Note: Joanna Southcott (1750-1814). Founder of a religious cult. On her death she left a box, purportedly containing prophecies, to be opened at a time of national crisis, in the presence of all the bishops of England. It was eventually opened in 1928, in the presence of a single bishop, and found to contain miscellaneous scraps of paper of little interest

VI.B.25.149 [075 in *JJA*]

(a) **^{r}joyshots**

MS 47472-121, LMA: in a quiet English garden ^+where the joyshots rang no more+^ | *JJA* 45:172 | Nov-Dec 1923 | I.3§<u>1.*2</u>/2.*2/3.*2 | *FW* 000.00

(b) **poker used**

(c) **Sunniest chapter**

(d) **v Their Majesties' enemies**

(e) **Boys v Fathers (cricket**

(f) [r]**Skittled out**

Note: Skittle out. To bowl out a batsman.
MS 47471b-65, LMS: Search me, the ~~other~~ ^+incapable+^ said ^+& in he ~~shot~~ ^+skittled+^+^. | *JJA* 47:361 | Jan 1924 | I.7§1.*1 | *FW* 187.01

(g) **The story begins**

(h) [b]**an Italian Excellency**

MS 47472-98, ILA: the ~~second gun~~ ^+two scatterguns+^ being ~~the syndic~~ ^+Michael Manning protosyndic+^ of ~~Drogheda~~ ^+Waterford+^ ^+and an Italian excellency+^ | *JJA* 45:005 | Aug-Sep 1923 | I.2§1.*1 | *FW* 031.20

(i) [r]**the pleasure of the morrow**

MS 47482b-30v, LPA: ^+what is our miserable today compared beside the pleasure of the morrow+^ | *JJA* 57:062 | May 1924 | III§1A.*2/1D.*2//2A.*2/2C.*2 | *FW* 455.25-6

(j) [r]**passed away /to/ the Beyond / by means of poison**

MS 47471b-2v, MT: Treacle Tom passed away painlessly in a state of nature | *JJA* 45:137 | Nov 1923 | I.3§1.*0 | *FW* 049.23

(k) **keep my wicket up**

Note: Wicket. The use of this unit in *FW* suggests cricket terminology, such as 'keeping wicket' (the wicket keeper being the player who stands behind the wicket, who can dismiss the batsman either by catching the ballafter he has hit it or by stumping him when he is out of his ground). This is not a technical term, but probably a nonce phrase, taken from a sports report.
MS 47482b-113v, LPA: our public at large appreciates it most highly of me that I am cleanliving [...] ^+as I ~~always~~ ^+perpetually+^ kept my wicket up.+^ | *JJA* 58:094 | Nov-Dec 1924 | III§3B.*2 | *FW* 532.17-18

(l) [r]**as you all know**

MS 47482b-113v, LPA: ^+^+by whom+^ as you all know [...] one of the ambitions of my ~~early~~ youth [...] I was confirmed in bed by one beloved curate [...]+^ | *JJA* 58:094 | Nov-Dec 1924 | III§3B.*2 | *FW* 533.24

(m) [r]**one of the ambitions of / my early youth (SP) I was / confirmed in bed**

Note: The sacrament of confirmation is intended to strengthen the faith of baptized persons. It is usually administered by a bishop, who anoints the candidates with chrism. Up to the 13C it was administered as soon as possible after baptism, but later the age was moved to twelve and then to ten. There are various stories of child saints, suffering from debilitating diseases, who were given the sacrament at lower ages and in their sickbeds.
MS 47482b-113v, LPA: ^+^+by whom+^ as you all know ^+of a child+^ ^+, dear humans,+^ one of the ambitions of my ~~early~~ youth ^+of a child from an early pea period+^ I was confirmed in bed by one beloved curate [...]+^ | *JJA* 58:094 | Nov-Dec 1924 | III§3B.*2 | *FW* 533.25-8

(n) **clothyard arrows**

Irish Independent 4 Aug 1923-5/3: [The Bow and Arrow in History / And its Place in Sport] The long-bow was five feet, and its shaft a clothyard; and this weapon in the hands of a Welshman penetrated an oak door four inches thick, and stood out a handbreadth on the other side, at Abergavenny in 1182.
Note: Clothyard. The yard by which cloth was measured: chiefly in 'cloth-yard shaft', applied in ballads to an arrow of the long bow. This is now the statute yard of 36 inches (*OED*).

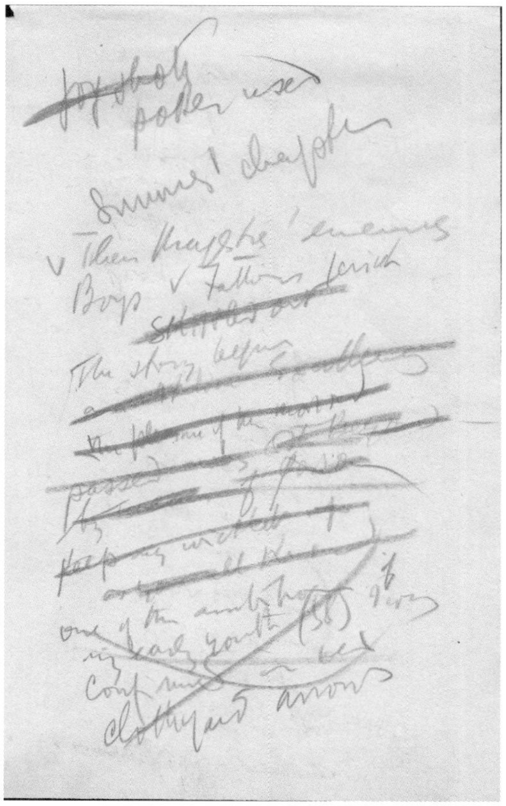

VI.B.25.149 [075 in *JJA*]

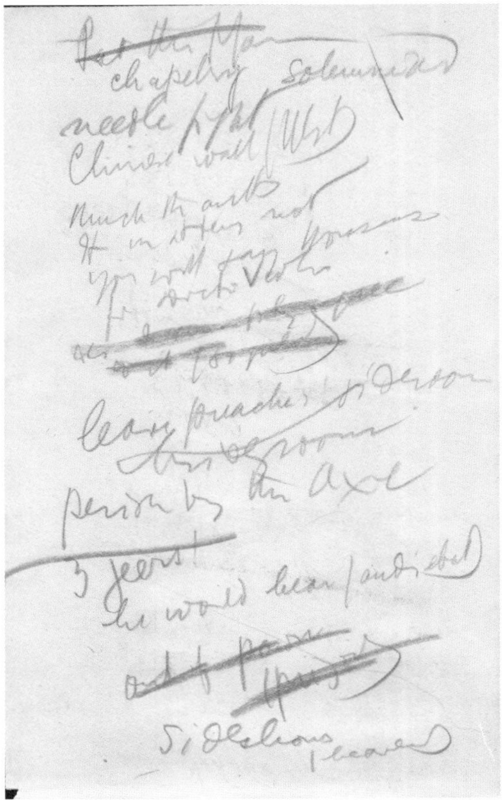

VI.B.25.150 [076 in *JJA*]

VI.B.25.150 [076 in *JJA*]

(a) **[r]Pat the Man**

MS 47471b-83v, LPA: the cornerboys burning his guy ^+& Pat the Man raising a laugh […]+^ | *JJA* 48:024 | Feb 1924 | I.8§1A.*1/1B.*1 | *FW* 205.29

(b) **chapelry**

Note: Chapelry. The parish attached to a chapel, or a division within a large parish having its own chapel.

(c) **solemnized**

Note: Entered on the right of the last unit.

(d) **needle fight**

Note: Needle fight. The *OED* gives this as an alternative form of 'needle match', which it defines as 'a match or contest that arouses much interest and excitement; a crucial or keenly fought match; a contest in which the contestants have a grudge against each other; a dispute.' The earliest citation is 1927.

(e) **Chinese wall (Ulst)**

Note: At the time of the Ango-Irish treaty, the status of Northern Ireland was particularly controversial and the press often compared the border to the Wall of China.

(f) **Much thanks**

(g) **It matters not**

(h) **You will say /nonsense/**

(i) **for Doctor /Victor/**

(j) **[r]as I simply agree / to it ~**

MS 47471b-32, MT: I will not have a reptile the like of McGrath Bros ^+[…]+^ to be spreading his ^+dirty+^ lies all round where we live as I simply agree to it, the obnoxious liar | *JJA* 46:257 | Dec 1923 | I.5§2.*0 | 'The Revered Letter' *FDV* 082.05-6

(k) **[r](signed)**

MS 47471b-33, MT: Hoping […] you will enjoy perusal and completely/ (Signed) | *JJA* 46:259 | Dec 1923 | I.5§2.*0 | 'The Revered Letter' *FDV* 083.08

(l) **leave preacher's sideroom / bridegroom**

(m) **perish by the Axe**

(n) **[r]3 jeers!**

MS 47474-25v, TsLPA: ^+[…] and another moment giving 3 jeers for his rotten little ghost of a Peppybeg,[…] +^ | *JJA* 47:404 | Apr-May 1925 | I.7§1.3/2.3 | *FW* 173.26

Note: FW 117.23 derives from VI.B.14.191(j).

(o) **he would hear (audiebat)**

Note: L. *Audiebat*. He would (continuously) hear.

(p) **[r]out of pawn / (prison)**

Note: See Eric Partridge, *Dictionary of the Underworld,* 'pawned': Imprisoned; in prison: since the 1920's.
MS 47471b-6, ILA: It was two coves of the name of Treacle Tom ^+as was just out of pawn+^ | *JJA* 45:035 | Oct 1923 | I.2§2.*1 | [*FW* 039.16]

(q) **side/shows/ / (heaven)**

VI.B.25.151 [077 in *JJA*]

(a) **interpleaded**

Note: Interplead. Legal term applied to cases where an individual is exposed to the adverse claims of two opposite parties, each requiring him/her to pay a certain sum of money, or deliver certain goods, and he/she is unable to comply because a reasonable doubt exists as to which of them is the rightful claimant. In such cases the claimants may be interpleaded: compelled to litigate the claim between themselves.

(b) **(Lascar)**

Note: Lascar. 1. An East Indian sailor. 2. An East Indian army servant. 3. A low grade East Indian artilleryman in the British Army.

(c) **a Pom(eranian)**

Note: Pom. A common abbreviation of Pomeranian dog.

(d) **cooper with 2 doz / of stout in a pigstye**

(e) **^{r}1000 % (A.G.)**

Note: A.G. Arthur Guinness.
Not located in MS/*FW*

(f) **street trading**

(g) **Jas**

(h) **^{r}boys’ 1^{d} flutter**

Evening Standard 24 July 1923-1/1: Betting Inquiry [...] L. C. C. Schoolmistress on Boys’ “Flutters” / Schoolboys’ 1^{d} Bets [...] / Remarkable allegations as to betting among schoolboys were made before the Betting Inquiry to-day by an assistant mistress in one of the L. C. C. schools for boys [...] The witness said that [...] she discovered on the day of the Lincoln Handicap that certain boys in her school had bets on the race.

Note: L. C. C. London County Council (now defunct).

MS 47471b-2, MT: during a priestly flutter | *JJA* 45:027 | Oct 1923 | I.2§2.*0 | *FW* 039.01

Note: The present cancellation was probably made in order to avoid reduplication with VI.B.11.003 ‘priestly flutters’, also crossed in red, which is the primary source of this entry.

(i) **^{r}young Dublin**

MS 47471b-8, ILS: ranging from slips of ~~boys~~ ^+young Dublins+^ with pocketed hands | *JJA* 45:037 | Oct 1923 | I.2§2.*1 | *FW* 042.29-30

(j) **cardigan**

(k) **chargeable to the parish**

(l) **the Broads**

?*Daily Mail* 23 July 1923-5/2: [The Romantic Broads] Now that the holiday season is with us, many readers will welcome such a book as Mr. W. A. Dutt’s “A Guide to the Norfolk Broads” (Methuen, 6s.).

Note: The Broads. The system of inland waterways in Norfolk, England, consisting of shallow lakes formed by the broadening of the Rivers Bure and Yare.

(m) **pro tanto**

Note: L. *Pro tanto*. For so much; to such an extent.

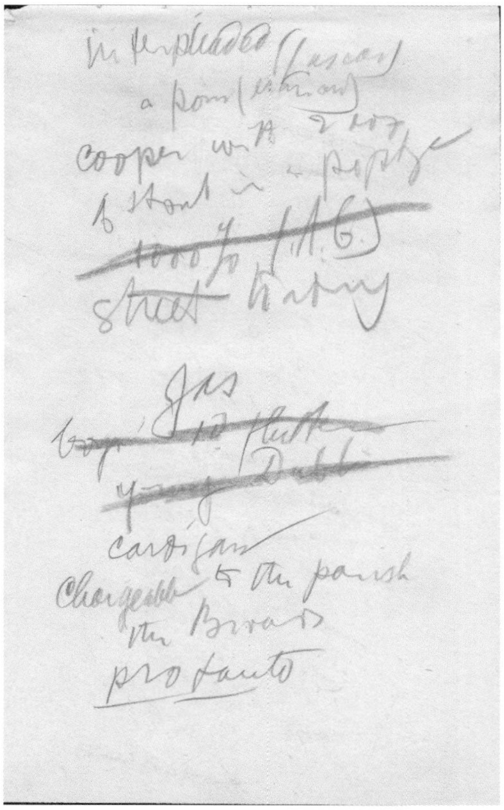

VI.B.25.151 [077 in *JJA*]

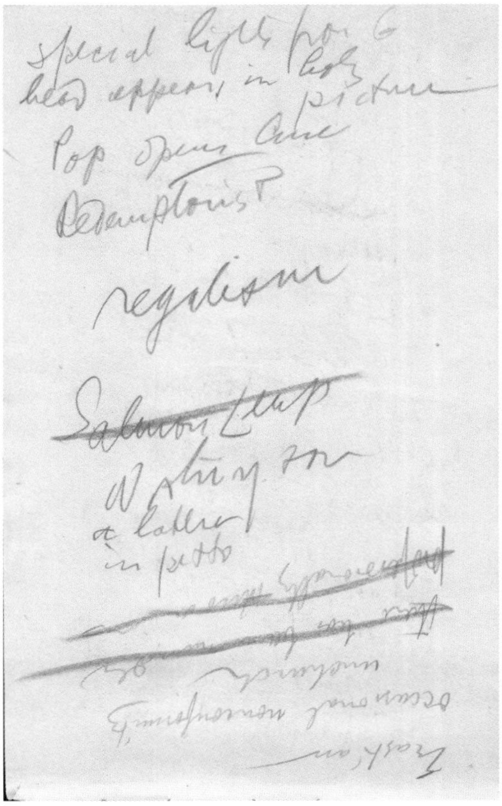

VI.B.25.152 [078 in *JJA*]

VI.B.25.152 [078 in *JJA*]

Note: Entries (k)-(m) upside down.

(a) **special lights from G / head appears in holy / picture**

(b) **Pop opens Cine**

(c) **Redemptorist**

Note: Redemptorist. A missionary priest of the congregation founded in 1732 by St. Alfonsus Liguori (1696-1787) for work among the poor.

(d) **regalism**

Note: Regalism: The doctrine or practice of the supremacy of the sovereign in ecclesiastical matters (*OED*).

(e) [r]**Salmon Leap**

Note: Salmon Leap. A former waterfall of the Liffey in Leixlip (a Scandinavian name, also meaning 'salmon leap') before the recent construction of a dam.

MS 47472-133, ILA: Earwicker ^+, who previous to that semidetached life had been known to eat his own length in rainbow trout,+^ was ^+, like the salmon of his ladderleap,+^ secretly feeding on his own misplaced fat. | *JJA* 46:023 | Dec 1923 | I.4§1A.*2 | *FW* 079.11-12

(f) **/Watington/**

(g) **a latere**

Note: L. *A latere*. From the side. The term is usually applied to a particular type of papal legate, a cleric sent on a mission by the Pope as his personal representative. See VI.B.14.134(k).

(h) **in petto**

Note: It. *In petto*. In the breast, in the heart. At times the Pope declares that in addition to those whom he has publicly made cardinals, he has made one or more others whose names he reserves *in petto*. When these are subsequently made known, they take rank from the date of their original nomination.

(i) **Erastian**

Note: Erastian. Pertaining to the doctrines of the 16C Swiss theologian Erastus. His actual concern was the tyrannic use of excommunication by the Calvinist churches, but he became popularly associated with the subordination of the ecclesiastical to the secular power. See (e).

(j) **occasional nonconformity**

Note: Occasional conformity. Conformity was compliance with the rites of the Church of England, necessary to qualify one for office. The practice of those who received the Sacrament according to the rites of the Church of England and who later, during their office, were present at any dissenting meeting for worship, was known as 'occasional conformity'.

(k) **unchurch**

Note: Unchurch. To expel from a church or from church membership; excommunicate.

(l) [r]**there has been /murder/**

MS 47471b-35, MT: and this go no mistake there had been real murder, | *JJA* 46:053 | Dec 1923 | I.4§2.*1 | *FW* 099.27

(m) [r]**professionally known /as/**

MS 47471b-39v, LPA: ^+ […] was rather put out […] about the thugs got up for McGrath by Sully. I am told that he is at present in hospital […] That he may never come out but he is a rattling fine bootmaker by profession+^ | *JJA* 46:268 | Dec 1923 | I.5§2.*1 | 'The Revered Letter' [→] MS 47488-124, MT: ~~M.G.~~ ^+Sully+^ is from all he drunk though he is a rattling fine bootmaker in his profession | *JJA* 63:193 | IV§4.*0 | Sep-Oct 1938 [*FW* 618.36-619.01]

VI.B.25.153 [079 in *JJA*]

Note: Entries on this page are upside down.

(a) **[r]Pop (Maundy)**

Note: Traditionally, on Maundy Thursday, alms, or 'maundy money', is distributed among the poor.

MS 47471b-86v, LPA: everytime she'd dip in her ~~bag~~ ^+sack+^ ^+& out with her maundy money+^ | *JJA* 48:030 | Feb 1924 | I.8§1A.*1/1B.*1 | *FW* 210.02

(b) **Kevineen >**

MS 47488-24v, MT: As an infant ^+~~The little stranger~~ ^+Shortly after him coming into the world+^+^ Kevineen delighted himself by playing with the sponge | *JJA* 63:038b | Jul 1923 | IV§2.*1 | *FDV* 276.04

MS 47471b-88, MT: ~~a~~ ^+the+^ flag of the saints & stripes for Kevineen O'Dea | *JJA* 48:033 | Feb 1924 | I.8§1A.*1/1B.*1 | *FW* 210.14

(c) **(9 names)**

Note: Kevin is given nine attributes ('poor Kevin' etc.) as part of the ninefold structure of the Kevin episode (*FW* 605.04-606.12).

(d) **[r]incensed (Kev)**

MS 47482b-21v, LPA: Shaun replied, ^+naturally very incensed,+^ | *JJA* 56:032 | May 1924 | III§1A.*2/1D.*2//2A.*2/2C.*2 | *FW* 412.14

(e) **passion**

(f) **O.L. of Red. of Captives**

Note: Order of Our Lady of the Redemption of Captives. A religious order, also known as the Mercedarians, founded in 1218 by St Peter Nolasco, to ransom Christians held as captives in Moorish Spain. Units (g)-(i) are probably taken from the same source.

(g) **clerical habits**

Note: See (f).

(h) **Eng. conv to Islam**

Note: See (f).

(i) **lay chain of food depots**

Note: See (f).

(j) **[g]command a full / view**

MS 47485-32, ILS: Is it not that we ~~have~~ ^+are commanding+^ from ~~here back~~ ^+fullback+^, woman permitting, a profusely fine birdseye view from beauhind this park. | *JJA* 60:260 | Mar-Apr 1926 | III§4.*2 | *FW* 564.06-8

(k) **Doggett's Coat & Bad**

Note: Doggett's Coat and Badge. One of the world's oldest continuing rowing races, held annually in England along the River Thames from London Bridge to Chelsea. Instituted in 1715 by Thomas Doggett, an English comic actor, who provided for a cash prize and 'an Orange coloured Livery with a Badge representing Liberty' to be awarded to the winner.

(l) **Bleck Co to white 1—**

(m) **Thames Conservancy**

Note: The Thames Conservancy Board has controlled the freshwater Thames since 1857 (the tidal Thames below Teddington is controlled by the Thames Water Authority).

(n) **fissiparous tendency**

Note: Fissiparous. Pertaining to reproduction by fission.

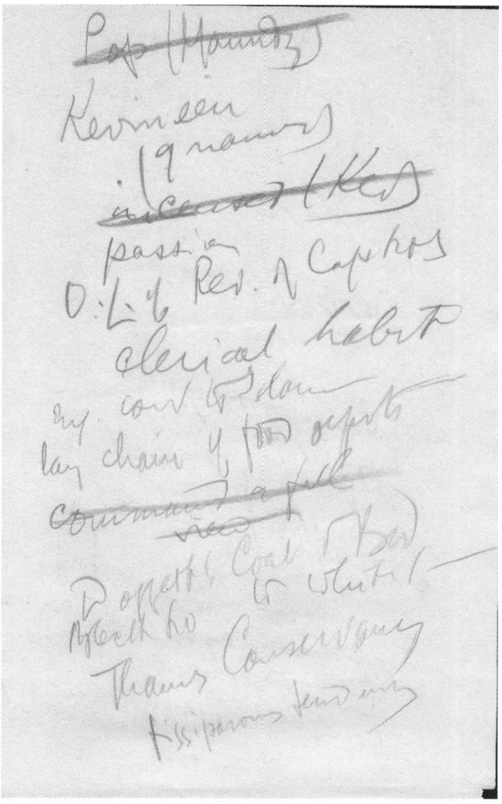

VI.B.25.153 [079 in *JJA*]

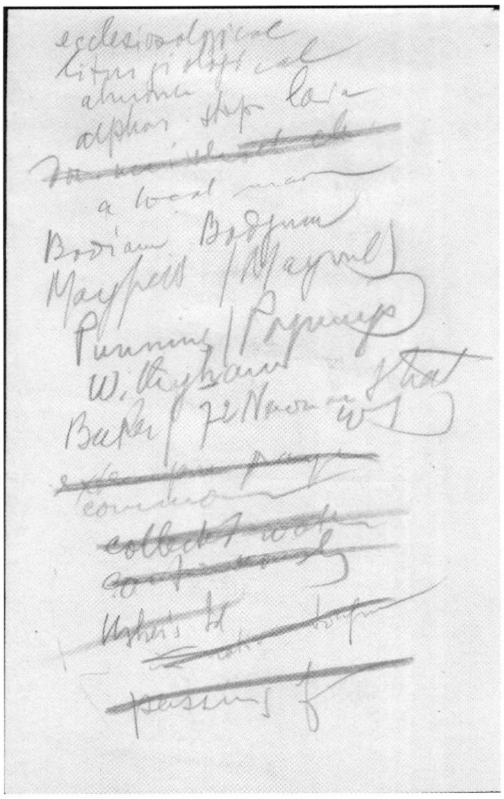

VI.B.25.154 [080 in *JJA*]

VI.B.25.154 [080 in *JJA*]

Note: Entries on this page are upside down.

(a) **ecclesiosological**

Note: Ecclesiological. Pertaining to ecclesiology, the science relating to the church or to churches.

(b) **liturgiological**

Note: Liturgiological. Pertaining to liturgiology, the science of liturgy.

(c) **almoner**

Note: Almoner. An official distributor of the alms of another. The name of a functionary in the house of a bishop, prince or person of rank.

(d) **alphas stop lava**

(e) [r]**doc universal ch**

MS 47488-26, BMA: venerated doctor solitarius ^+of the universal church+^ | *JJA* 60:038d | Jul 1923 | IV§2.*3 | *FW* 606.08

(f) **a local man**

(g) **Bodiam Bodjum / Mayfield (Mayvul) / Punnins (Poynings) / Withyham / Baker (72 Newman Street / W1)**

Note: The website http://homepages.rootsweb.com/~surnamru/steve/sussexpronounce.html, gives extracts from a booklet called *East Sussex Place Names* by 'An Old-Fashioned Man' published in 1920. A number of East Sussex town and village names are listed, each followed by the Sussex or local pronunciation. The following are included:

Bodiam – Bodjum […] Mayfield – Mayvul […] Poynings – Punnins […]

Withyham, at (j) above, is presumably on the list from which Joyce's notes derived. This is probably some review of the book rather than the book itself. The name and London address above are probably an agency where the book can be bought.

(h) [r]**extempore prayer**

MS 47488-26, BMA: ^+, memory ^+extempore+^ proposing ad intellect ^+formally+^ considering, recluse,+^ | *JJA* 63:038d | Jul 1923 | IV§2.*3 | *FW* 606.09

(i) **common**

(j) [r]**collected water / continuously**

MS 47488-26, ILS: ~~filled~~ ^+collected+^ with Gregorian water | *JJA* 63:038d | Jul 1923 | IV§2.*3 | *FW* 605.30

(k) [g]**Usher's Isl**

Note: Usher's Island. A quay on the south side of the Liffey, near the Phoenix Park. Well-known as the location of the home of the Misses Morkan, in 'The Dead'.
MS 47474-176, TsILS: she ~~multiplied~~ ^+ushered ~~out~~ round+^ a thousand isles and islets dun all over her little mary. | *JJA* 48:126 | Jul 1925 | I.8§1.5' | *FW* 206.35

(l) [r]**in native tongue**

MS 47472-137, ILA: the same ^+native+^ language | *JJA* 46:028 | Dec 1923 | I.4§1A.*2 | *FW* 000.00

(m) [r]**passing of**

MS 47471b-9v, MT: with the passing of years | *JJA* 45:140 | Nov 1923 | I.3§1.*1 | *FW* 051.02

VI.B.25.155 [081 in *JJA*]

Note: Entries (f)-(i) are upside down.

(a) [b]**fullbottom wig**

Note: Full-bottom wig. A wig having a full or large bottom.
MS 47481-3v, ILA: Justice Squelchman ^+in her ^+fullbottom+^ wig & beard+^ | *JJA* 56:032 | Oct 1923 | II.4§2.*0/3A.*1 | *FW* 390.36

(b) **Finn's Hotel**

Note: Finn's Hotel. Former hotel, in Clare Street, Dublin, where Nora Barnacle worked when first encountered by Joyce. See 156(c).

(c) [r]**Ginger Jane / (car)**

MS 47472-124, LMA: who was hosing his runabout ^+Ginger Jane+^, | *JJA* 45:175 | Nov-Dec 1923 | I.3§1.*2/2.*2/3.*2 | *FW* 059.25

(d) **Merton House / S. Bride's Ave / EC4**

Note: St. Bride's Avenue is in London EC4, but no Merton House has so far been traced.

(e) [r]**if it cd speak**

Not located in MS/*FW*

(f) [o]**Saltings**

MS 47472-34, LMA: ^+where wone and wail whimbrel ^+~~to~~ and peewee+^ o'er the Saltings where will be citie ^+by law of isthmon,+^ where ^+by ~~dr~~ a droit of signory+^ icefloe was+^ | *JJA* 44:122 | Nov-Dec 1926 | I.1§1.*2/2.*2 | *FW* 017.20

(g) **church served by priests**

(h) **stance**

(i) **backboard**

VI.B.25.155 is reproduced in colour at the end of this volume

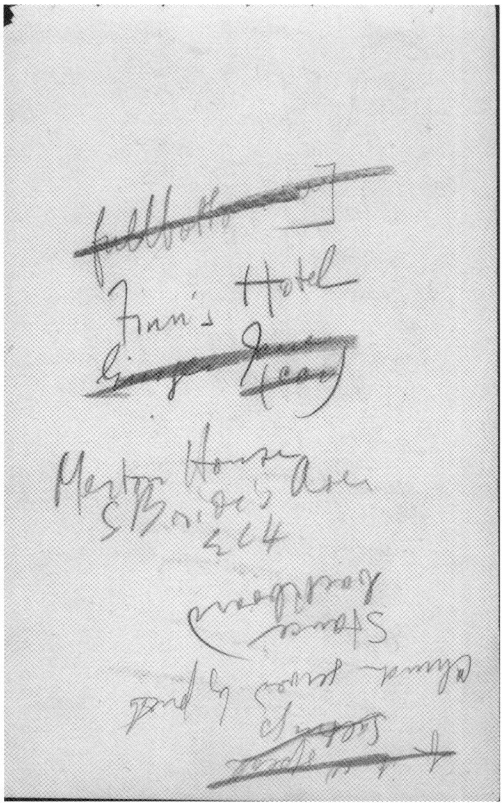

VI.B.25.155 [081 in *JJA*]

VI.B.25.156 [082 in *JJA*]

(a) **trousers hung perfect**

(b) **happy feet**

(c) **Finn's Hotel / House that Finn Built**

Note: See 155(b).

(d) **went to U S to beg the / Irish question**

(e) **I have /hear/ W for / quite a while**

(f) **they rifle wardrobes**

Note: A line joins this entry to 'Finn's Hotel' at (c).

(g) **adding machines**

(h) **/Moron (Soleilland)/**

(i) **Kingpin / (hotel bar)**

(j) [r]**dinkum**

Note: Australian. Dinkum. 1. Work, toil. 2. Honest, true, thorough. See 157(n).
MS 47471b-29v, MT: where is ~~he who is the man~~ ^+the bright soandso who is able+^ to give us the dinkum oil? | *JJA* 46:232 | Dec 1923 | I.5§1.*0 | *FW* 108.28

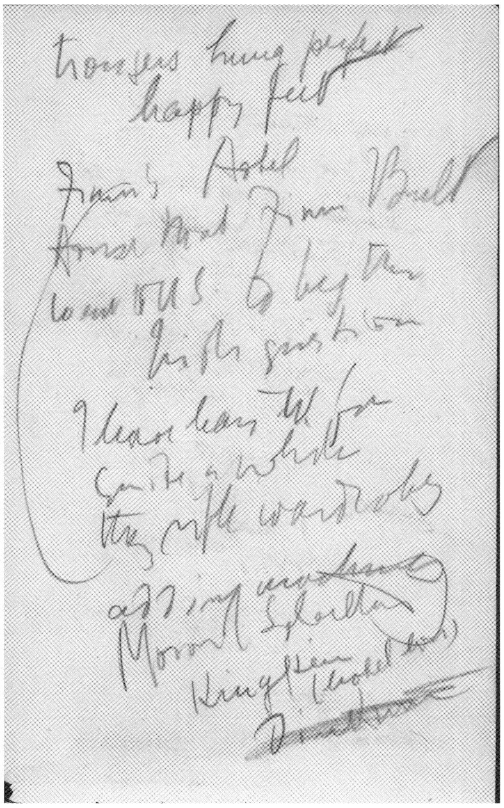

VI.B.25.156 [082 in *JJA*]

VI.B.25.156 and VI.B.25.157 are reproduced in colour at the end of this volume

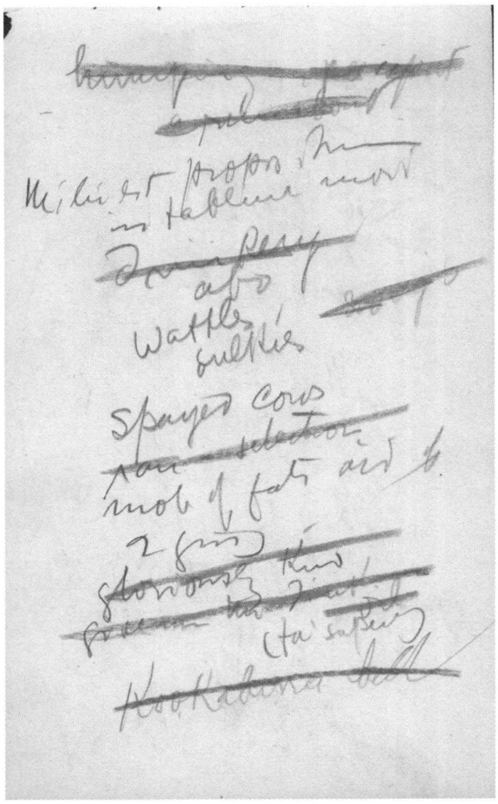

VI.B.25.157 [083 in *JJA*]

VI.B.25.157 [083 in *JJA*]

(a) ^{r}**humping a /passport/**

MS 47471b-13, MT: One tall man ~~carr~~ humping a suspicious parcel when returning late | *JJA* 45:155 | Nov 1923 | I.3§2.*1 | *FW* 062.28

(b) ^{r}**a runabout**

Note: Runabout. A small, light car.

MS 47472-124, MT: A more than usually sober taxidriver, who was hosing his ^+Ginger Jane+^runabout | *JJA* 45:175 | Nov-Dec 1923 | I.3§1.*2/2.*2/3.*2 | *FW* 059.25

(c) **Nihilist proposition**

(d) **in tableau most**

(e) ^{r}**drunkery**

Note: Sl. Drunkery. A public-house or drink-shop. A place to get drunk in.

MS 47471b-60, BMA: a drug ^+& drunkery+^ addict megalomane | *JJA* 47:351 | Jan 1924 | I.7§1.*1 | *FW* 179.20

(f) **abo**

Note: Abo. See entry in Partridge's *Dictionary of Slang and Unconventional English* (8th edition): 'Abo. Australian Aboriginal: Aus. coll.: mid C.19-20. Wilkes. "Not always intended as derogatory, but now [1977] increasingly taken to be so."'

(g) **wattles**

Note: Wattle. Acacia trees were used by early Australian settlers to build wattle-and-daub dwellings and became known as 'wattles'. 'Wattle Day' is an Australian national holiday, held on 1 August or 1 September, depending on the flowering of the wattle in different states. See alsoVI.B.10.116(k).

(h) ^{r}**swags**

Note: Entered in right margin.

Swag. A wreath or festoon of flowers or foliage. The pack or bundle containing the personal belongings of a swagman, an Australian tramp.

MS 47471b-31, MT: I hereafter swear he never once sent out the swags with a drop | *JJA* 46:255 | Dec 1923 | I.5§2.*0 | 'The Revered Letter' [→] MS 47488-116v, MT: the man what never put a drop in the swags but milk from a natural cows | *JJA* 63:182 | IV§4.*0 | Sep-Oct 1938 | *FW* 615.27

(i) **sulkies**

Note: Sulky. Probably a light two-wheeled carriage for one person, used for races between trotting horses.

VI.A.0041 ('Araby'): 'sulkies'.

(j) **spayed cows**

Note: Spay. To remove the ovaries of a female animal, preventing reproduction.

(k) ^{r}**ran selection**

MS 47482b-115, LMA: I will say that since ^+I ran a selection here+^ ^+where+^ my toils of domestication began famine has receded from this land. | *JJA* 58:097 | Nov-Dec 1924 | III§3B.*2 | *FW* 539.21-2

(l) **mob of fats aid of / 2 gins**

(m) ^{r}**gloriously kind**

MS 47482b-32, TMA: You are most ^+gloriously+^ kind as ever, dear relative, | *JJA* 57:065 | April 1926 | III§1A.*2/1D.*2//2A.*2/2C.*2 | *FW* 461.36

(n) **[r]give me the dinkum / oil**

Note: Australian. The dinkum oil. The truth. See 156(k)
MS 47471b-29v, MT: ~~he who is the man~~ ^+the bright soandso who is able+^ to give us the dinkum oil? | *JJA* 46:232 | Dec 1923 | I.5§1.*0 | *FW* 108.28

(o) **(fa's super)**

Note: ?English upper class colloquial. Fa. Father.

(p) **[b]Kookaburra bell**

Note: Kookaburra. Native Australian name for the brown kingfisher, also known as the laughing jackass, on account of its laughing cry.
MS 47481-5, TMA: they used to be getting up ^+at the Kookaburra bell+^ | *JJA* 56:036 | Oct 1923 | II.4§2.*0/3A.*1 | *FW* 393.26

VI.B.25.158 [084 in *JJA*]

Note: Entries on this page are upside down.

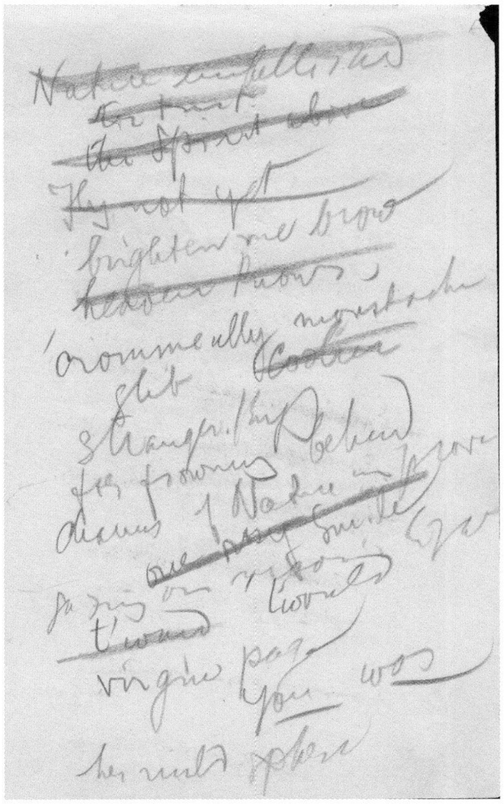

VI.B.25.158 [084 in *JJA*]

(a) **[r]Nature embellished / the tint**

Moore's Melodies: ['Remember the Glories of Brien the Brave'] Mononia! When Nature embellish'd the tint / Of thy fields
MS 47481-95, LMA: The sea ^of a pure tint embellished by nature^ looked awfully pretty | *JJA* 56:008 | Apr 1923 | II.4§1.*1 | *FW* 386.01

(b) **[r]the Spirit above**

Moore's Melodies: ['When he, who adores thee'] In my last humble prayer to the Spirit above, / Thy name shall be mingled with mine,
MS 47482b-33, BMA: who will ~~pray fervently~~ ^+fervently ^+to the Spirit Above+^ pray+^| *JJA* 57:067 | May 1924 | III§1A.*2/1D.*2//2A.*2/2C.*2 | *FW* 472.32

(c) **[o]Fly not yet**

Moore's Melodies: [Title] 'Fly not yet'
MS 47472-25, MT: Cry not yet! There's many a smile to Nondum, with sytty maids per man, sir, and the park's so dark by kindlelight. | *JJA* 44:128 | Nov 1926 | I.1§1.*2/2.*2 | *FW* 020.19

(d) **brighten me brow**

Moore's Melodies: ['Oh! think not my spirits are always as light'] Nor expect that the heart-beaming smile of tonight / Will return with to-morrow to brighten my brow.

(e) **[r]heaven knows,**

Moore's Melodies: ['Oh! think not my spirits are always so light'] The thread of our life would be dark, Heaven knows!
MS 47481-95v, ILA: No, ^+heaven knows,+^ far from it | *JJA* 56:011 | Apr 1923 | II.4§1.*1 | *FW* 396.22

(f) **crommeally moustache >**

(g) **glib [r]Coolin >**

MS 47481-95, LMA: By elevation of ^+unyawning+^ eyelids ^+~~to~~ ^+t'ward+^ her dear coolin+^ | *JJA* 56:009 | Apr 1923 | II.4§1.*1 | *FW* 000.00

(h) **stranger (Eng) >**

(i) **foes frowning behind**

Moore's Melodies: ['Though the last glimpse of Erin' (Coulin)] 'To the gloom of some desert, or cold rocky shore, / Where the eye of the stranger can haunt us no more, / I will fly with my Coulin, and think the rough wind / Less rude

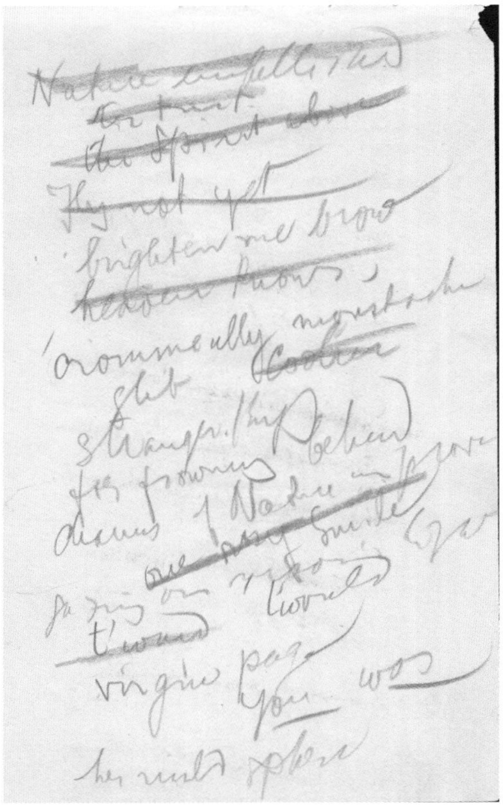

VI.B.25.158 [084 in *JJA*]

than the foes we leave frowning behind: -' Moore adds the following note: 'In the twenty-eighth year of the reign of Henry VIII, an Act was made respecting the habits and dress in general of the Irish, whereas all persons were restrained ... from wearing Glibbes, or Coulins (long locks), on their heads, or hair on the upper lip, called Crommeal. On this occasion a Song was written by one of our bards, in which an Irish virgin is made to give the preference to her dear Coulin (or the youth with the flowing locks), to all the strangers (by which the English were meant), or those who wore their habits. Of this song the Air alone has reached us, and is universally admired. [...]'—Walker's Historical Memoirs of Irish Bards, page 134.

(j) **charms of Nature improve**

Moore's Melodies: ['The meeting of the waters'] how the best charms of nature improve / When we see them reflected in looks that we love.

(k) **[r]one rosy Smile**

Moore's Melodies: ['St. Senanus and the lady'] But legends hint that had the maid / Till morning's light delayed; / And giv'n the saint one rosy smile, / She ne'er had left his lonely isle.'
MS 47482b-26v, LPA: goodwill girls, ^+~~while~~, who they were all making a tremendous fuss ~~about~~ ^+of +^him & his ~~rosy~~ ^+rosyposy+^ smile & smelling his nice perfume [...]+^ | *JJA* 57:054 | May 1924 | III§1A.*2/1D.*2//2A.*2/2C.*2 | *FW* 430.22

(l) **gazing on moon's light**

Moore's Melodies: [Title] 'While Gazing on the Moon's Light'

(m) **[r]t'ward ~**

?Moore's Melodies: ['Wreath the bowl'] We'll take a flight / Tow'rds heaven tonight
MS 47481-95, LMA: By elevation of ^+unyawning+^ eyelids ^+~~to~~ ^+t'ward+^ her dear coolin+^ | *JJA* 56:009 | Apr 1923 | 1 | *FW* 000.00

(n) **twould**

Moore's Melodies: ['How dear to me the hour'] And think 'twould lead to some bright isle of rest.

(o) **virgin page**

Moore's Melodies: [Title]: 'Take back the virgin page'

(p) **you was**

Not found in Moore's *Melodies*.

(q) **her mild sphere**

Moore's Melodies: ['While Gazing on the Moon's Light'] That mild sphere

VI.B.25.158 and VI.B.25.159 are reproduced in colour at the end of this volume

VI.B.25.159 [085 in *JJA*]

Note: Entries on this page are upside down.

(a) **[r]dimpling bliss**

Moore's Melodies: ['While Gazing on the Moon's Light'] (while / The moon's smile / Play'd o'er a stream, in dimpling bliss)
MS 47481-95v, ILA: ^+laughing at the same time delightfully ^+in dimpling bliss+^+^ | *JJA* 56:011 | Apr 1923 | II.4§1.*1 | *FW* 398.20

(b) **~~dim~~**

Note: Joyce began to write 'dimpling' again but then crossed it out.

(c) **bootleg instrument**

Not found in Moore's *Melodies*.

(d) **at his seat**

Not found in Moore's *Melodies*.

(e) **[r]rosecrumpler**

Moore's Melodies: ['Lesbia hath a beaming eye'] Bed of peace! whose roughest part / Is but the crumpling of the roses.
MS 47481-95, ILS: Nothing if not amorous ~~he~~ ^+he, the rosecrumpler,+^ then having dephlegmatised his guttur | *JJA* 56:009 | Apr 1923 | II.4§1.*1 | *FW* 395.16

(f) **[r]most unholy blue**

Moore's Melodies: ['By that Lake, whose gloomy shore'] 'Twas from Kathleen's eyes he flew, — / Eyes of most unholy blue!
MS 47481-95v, ILA: a firstrate pair of bedroom eyes ^+of most unholy hazel^+ | *JJA* 56:010 | Apr 1923 | II.4§1.*1 | *FW* 396.11

(g) **[r]bumpersprinkling**

Moore's Melodies: ['Fill the bumper fair'] Ev'ry drop we sprinkle
MS 47471-60v, LPS: Yet ~~he~~ ^+the bumpersprinkler+^ used to boast aloud to himself | *JJA* 47:352 | Jan 1924 | I.7§1.*1 | *FW* 180.34

(h) **[r]as slow their ship**

Moore's Melodies: [Title]: 'As slow our ship her foamy track'
MS 47481-95, TM: ^+As slow their ship+^ [...] The handsome ^+~~sunburnt~~ ^+brineburnt+^+^ 6 footer | *JJA* 56:008 | Apr 1923 | II.4§1.*1 | *FW* 383.20

(i) **/The curses force/**

Not found in Moore's *Melodies*.

(j) **thee, thee / only thee**

Moore's Melodies: [Title]: 'Thee, thee, only thee!'

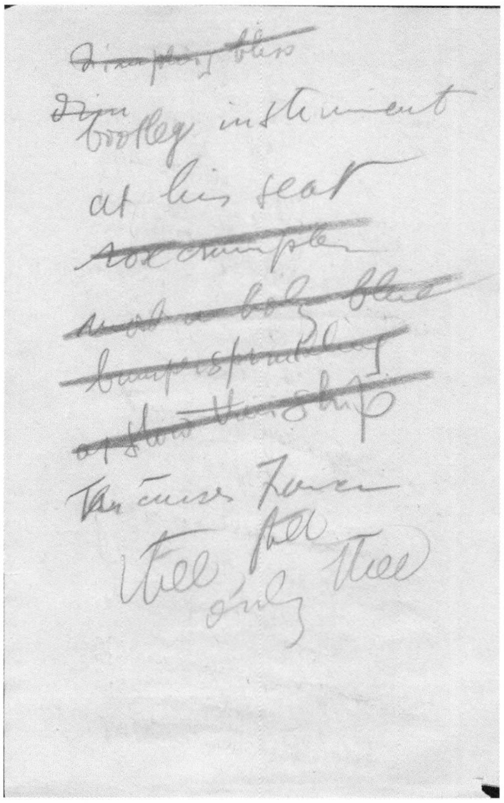

VI.B.25.159 [085 in *JJA*]

VI.B.25.160 [086 in *JJA*]

Note: Entries (a) to (n) are upside down.

(a) **[r]his trousers changed / colour**

MS 47471b-51v, MT: his face & trousers ~~changing~~ ^+changed+^ colour every time a ~~rifle spoke~~ ^+gat croaked.+^ | *JJA* 47:334 | Jan 1924 | I.7§1.*0 | *FW* 177.07

(b) **magpie takes ring from / /commode/ to shelf**

(c) **[r]Cash draper**

MS 47471b-6, ILA: a discharged ^+cash+^ ~~drapers~~ ^+draper's+^ executive | *JJA* 45:035 | Oct 1923 | I.2§2.*1 | *FW* 040.15

(d) **freakfr —**

(e) **no Eng saint since Luther**

(f) **at the pres. mom: You'd find / a boy — & he would / teach CSP**

Note: CSP. In Joyce's notes this usually denotes Charles Stuart Parnell.

(g) **[b]Southron**

Note: A native of the South of Great Britain, usually denoting an Englishman, as opposed to a native of Scotland.

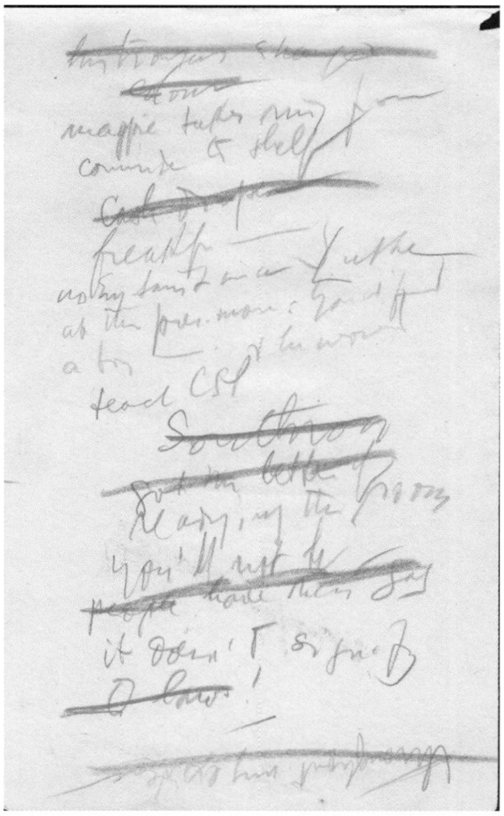

VI.B.25.160 [086 in *JJA*]

MS 47472-98v, ILS: that good and great ^+& no ordinary+^ ~~man~~ ^+Southron+^ Earwicker | *JJA* 45:007 | Aug-Sep 1923 | I.2§1.*1 | *FW* 034.13

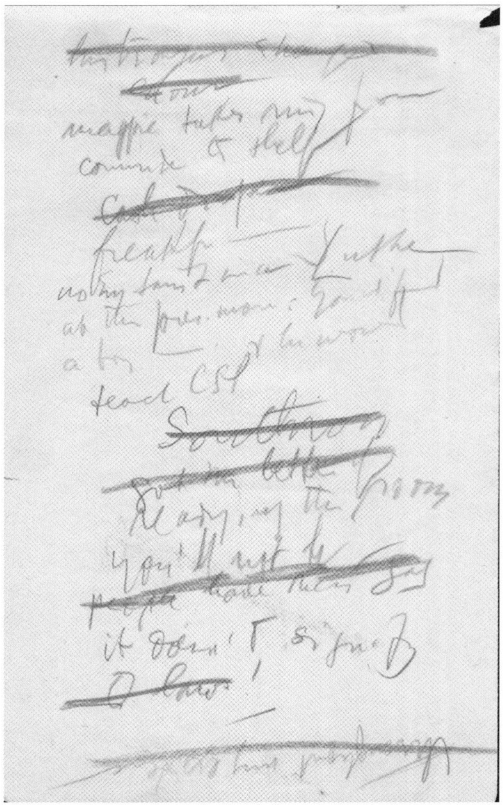

VI.B.25.160 [086 in *JJA*]

(h) [r]**got the better of**

MS 47471b-58v, LPA: eyes of Irish blue were smiling up their sleeves ^+rank funk getting the better of him,+^ the scut fled | *JJA* 47:348 | Jan 1924 | I.7§1.*1 | *FW* 176.26

(i) **readying the room**

(j) **you'll not be**

(k) [r]**people have their say**

Not located in MS/*FW*

(l) **it doesn't signify**

(m) [r]**O laws!**

Note: See also VI.B.10.088(b).
MS 47471b-82, LMS: O ~~my~~ ^+laws+^! | *JJA* 48:021 | Feb 1924 | I.8§1A.*1/1B.*1 | [*FW* 201.35]

(n) [b]**throughout my existence**

Note: See reproduction. This entry is at the top of the page and is *not* upside down.
MS 47472-98v, ILA: To anyone who knew and loved H.C. Earwicker ^+throughout his existence+^ | *JJA* 45:007 | Aug-Sep 1923 | I.2§1.*1 | *FW* 033.30-1

VI.B.25.161 [087 in *JJA*]

Note: Entries on this page are upside down.

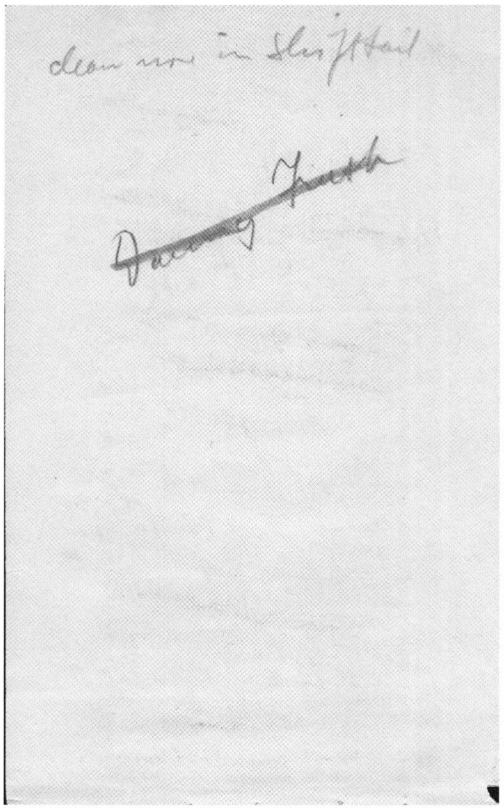

VI.B.25.161 [087 in *JJA*]

(a) **clean none in shifttail**

(b) [r]**Danny Frush**

Note: Danny Frush. A featherweight boxer, active 1917-26.

Frush. The thrush, or tender part of a horse's foot (*EDD*).

MS 47472-111, LMA: ^+, thanks to you, great little Danny Frush, who in his neverrip mud and purple surely unlike any other jockey that ever happened+^ | *JJA* 45:049 | Nov-Dec 1923 | I.2§2.*2/3*2 | *FW* 000.00

VI.B.25.162 [088 in *JJA*]

Note: Entries (e)-(j) are upside down.

(a) **City Hall 1769 / arch. Thos. Coaley >**

(b) **Exchange, 1852, O'Connell**

Freeman's Journal 30 July 1923-8/5: [By the Way] Now that the City Hall is about to resume its old associations with the Municipality as the meeting place of the Corporation, it is interesting […] to recall the fact that it was built from the designs of Thomas Coaley, in 1769, by a society of Dublin merchants […] It was then used as the "Exchange," but really became chiefly noted as a popular place for public meetings, and it was there that the famous Volunteers used to meet. Here, too, Dan O'Connell made his first public speech—a protest against the Union. It was in 1852 that the Exchange became the City Hall of the Corporation of Dublin.

(c) **Pine Forest, Rathfarnham**

?*Freeman's Journal* 10 August 1923-7/6: [In the Pine Forest / Dramatic Coup Near Dublin Recalled / Accused on Trial] The dramatic arrest of men "on the run" in the Pine Forest, Rathfarnham, was recalled in the Commission Court,

Green street, Dublin, yesterday when, before Mr. Justice Pim, William Lalor, John Costello and Christopher Carroll were indicted for having broken into the premises of Robert Kennedy, 26-7 Drury street, and stealing a quantity of clothing

Note: Rathfarnham village is four miles south of the centre of Dublin. The Pine Forest is further south, at the beginning of the Dublin Mountains.

(d) **[b]decorated by most / regal of belches**

MS 47480-270, BMA: ^+singing to himself through his ^+old+^ tears broken by regal belches […]+^ | *JJA* 55:446c | Jun 1923 | II.3§7.*2 | *FW* 381.21

(e) **jolly fine f—**

(f) **thanked**

(g) **her share of hair**

(h) **heart shook with pity**

VI.B.25.162 and VI.B.25.163 are reproduced in colour at the end of this volume

(i) **[r]in $\frac{1}{2}$ mourning**

?Evening Standard 10 Aug 1923-16/4: [Cowes in Half Mourning, / Regatta Change for Dead President. / Postponed Races. […]] Cowes is in semi-mourning to-day for President Harding's funeral, and every token of sympathy with the U.S. is indicated. / The big handicap race for yachts exceeding a hundred tons, in which the King's Britannia is entered, has been postponed until to-morrow, and to-day all yachts lying in the roadstead, including the Victoria and Albert, lowered their flags to half mast.

Note: Half-mourning. A period of mourning following the expiry of full mourning. Clothing during this period, when the black of full mourning is relieved by other colours.

MS 47485-33, LMA: In the sleepingchamber ^+^+The court to go into half morning.+^ […]+^. | *JJA* 60:261 | Mar-Apr 1926 | III§4.*2 | *FW* 566.07

(j) **[g]how unpardonable of me!**

MS 47485-31, LMA: But hush! ^+How unpardonable of me!+^ I beg ^+you+^ for your ~~pardon.~~ ^+venials.+^ Sincerely I do. | *JJA* 60:259 | Mar-Apr 1926 | III§4.*2 | *FW* 562.36

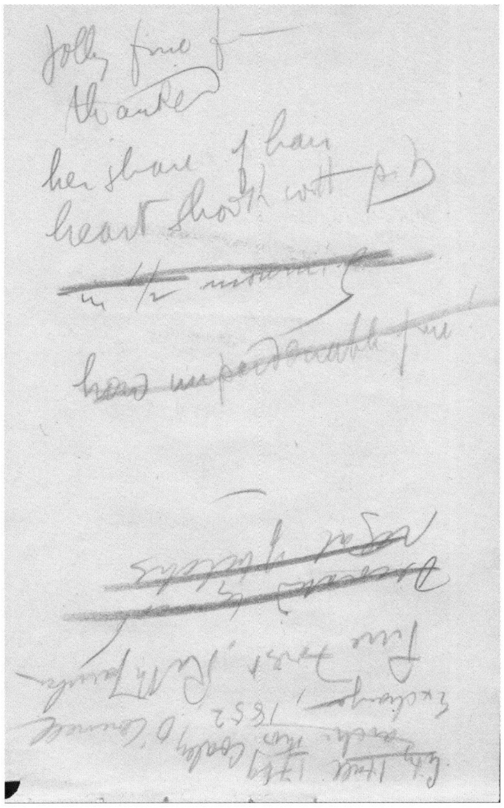

VI.B.25.162 [088 in *JJA*]

VI.B.25.163 [089 in *JJA*]

Note: Entries on this page are upside down.

(a) **H allow to /thrash/ if stick not / thicker than thumb**

Note: H. Husband.

(b) **4 ~~figs~~ tier aero**

(c) **it was nothing for him to eat**

(d) **Mesdames Naughty Forty & / Flighty Fifty**

(e) **[r]a crying shame**

MS 47471-12, MT: It would be a crying shame | *JJA* 45:147 | Nov 1923 | I.3§1.*1 | *FW* 060.05

(f) **[r]first class!**

MS 47482b-29v, LPA: ^+I'd never cry crack till I'd run my shoestring into near a million as a 1st class dealer & everything+^ | *JJA* 57:060 | May 1924 | III§1A.*2/1D.*2//2A.*2/2C.*2 | *FW* 451.34

(g) **full dress rehearsal**

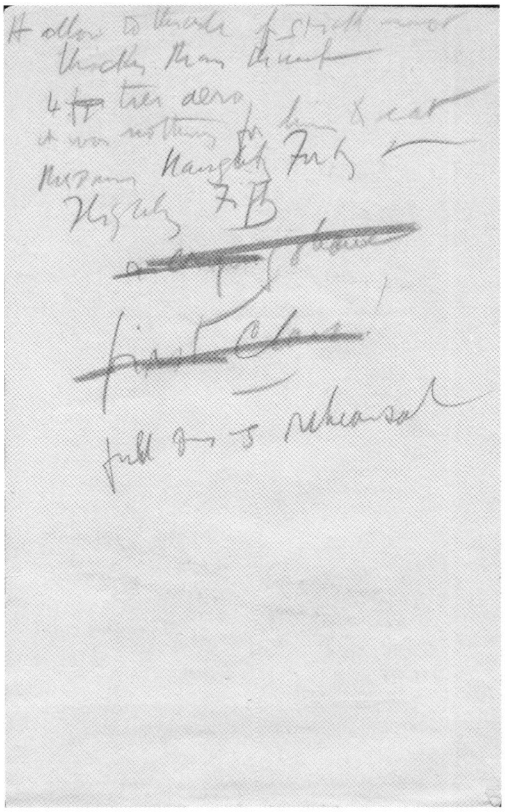

VI.B.25.163 [089 in *JJA*]

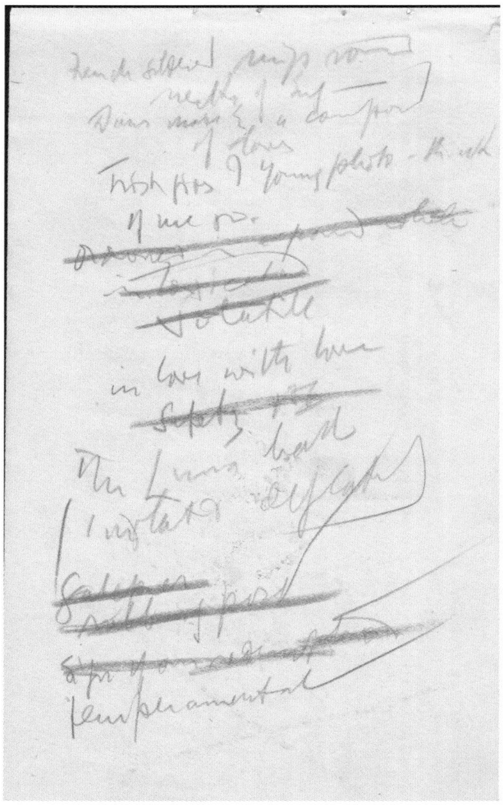

VI.B.25.164 [090 in *JJA*]

VI.B.25.164 [090 in *JJA*]

Note: Entries on this page are upside down.

(a) **French soldered rings round / necks of Eng —**

(b) **Danes make E a compound / of slaves**

(c) **Trist gives I young photo — think / of me so.**

(d) ^{r}**drowned in a pond while / intoxicated**

MS 47471b-27v, LPA: ^+He had walked into a pond while intoxicated up to that point where braced ~~meet buttons~~ ^+shirts meet knickerbockers+^+^ | *JJA* 46:046 | Nov-Dec 1923 | I.4§2.*0 | *FW* 098.20

(e) ^{r}**volatile**

MS 47481-95v, ILA: before the traditional 10 seconds were up ^+volatile+^ Brittany considerately allowed his farfamed ^+sparking plug+^ chokegrip to relax | *JJA* 56:011 | Apr 1923 | II.4§1.*1 | *FW* 396.29

(f) **in love with love**

(g) ^{r}**safety 1st**

MS 47481-95v, ILA: ^+believing in safety first,+^ after which before the traditional 10 seconds were up | *JJA* 56:011 | Apr 1923 | II.4§1.*1 | *FW* 000.00

(h) **the Luna ball (inflate & deflate)**

?*Evening Standard* 27 July 1923-7/2: [Luna Ball Mishap / Deptford Woman Awarded £1000 Damages] Miss Kathleen Sheehan, of Deptford, who claimed damages for injuries sustained while riding on the Luna Ball at Dreamland Park, Margate, was to-day awarded £1000 and costs by Mr. Justice Avory in the King's Bench Division against Dreamland (Margate) Ltd.[…] The Luna Ball was a sixpenny sideshow, and the amusement consisted of riding on a large ball which was inflated and deflated.

(i) ^{r}**gatepier**

Note: Pier. Each of the pillars or posts of a gate.
MS 47472-127, LMS: falling up against the ~~gate~~ ^+gatepier which he took for a rubbingpost with only peaceable intentions+^ | *JJA* 45:178 | Nov-Dec 1923 | I.3§1.*2/2.*2/3.*2 | *FW* 063.28

(j) ^{r}**rubbing post**

Note: Rubbing post. A post allowing an animal to rub itself.
MS 47472-127, LMS: falling up against the ~~gate~~ ^+gatepier which he took for a rubbingpost with only peaceable intentions+^ | *JJA* 45:178 | Nov-Dec 1923 | I.3§1.*2/2.*2/3.*2 | *FW* 000.00

(k) ^{r}**sign of our redemption**

Note: The Cross is traditionally seen as the 'sign of our redemption'.
MS 47471b-5, ILA: the monument ^+that sign of our redemption+^ | *JJA* 45:033 | Oct 1923 | I.2§2.*1 | *FW* 036.24-5

(l) **temperamental**

VI.B.25.165 [091 in *JJA*]

Note: Entries on this page are upside down.

(a) ^{r}**Needles & Pins / Blankets & Skins / When a man's married / His**

sorrow begins

Note: English proverbial phrase. See the *Oxford Dictionary of English Proverbs* for citations.

MS 47471-86v, LPA: a jigsaw puzzle ^+of needles & pins & blankets & skins+^ between them | *JJA* 48:030 | Feb 1924 | I.8§1A.*1/<u>1B.*1</u> | *FW* 210.11

(b) [r]**mental defective**

?*Freeman's Journal* 28 July 1923-3/1: [Mental Deficiency]

MS 47471b-52v, MT: Nabuchadonosor himself had not such a high & mighty opinion of himself as had this mental defective | *JJA* 47:336 | Jan 1924 | I.7§1.*0 | *FW* 177.16

(c) **Trist. Je will.**

(d) **druids & clerics grave / together, conv. gesticulate**

(e) [r]**at first blush**

MS 47481-95v, ILA: if the unvarnished truth must be told ^+at the very first blush+^ lovingly she lovegulped | *JJA* 56:011 | Apr 1923 | II.4§1.*1 | *FW* 000.00

(f) **the reds / — yellows (men)**

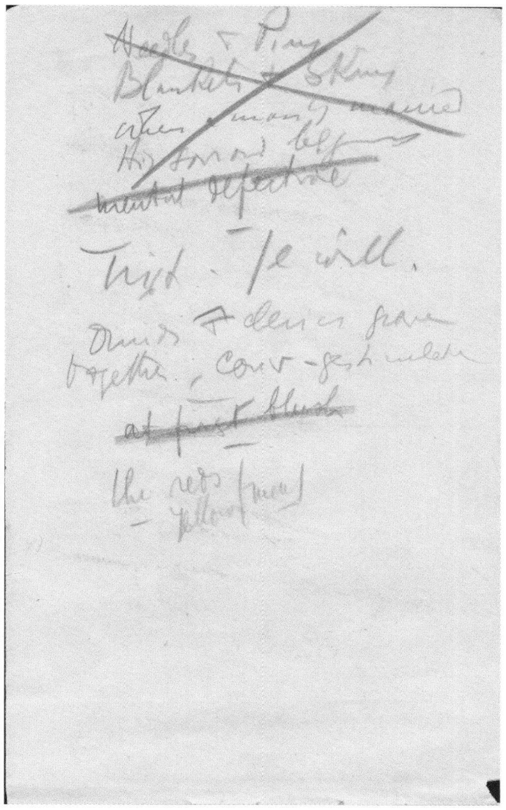

VI.B.25.165 [091 in *JJA*]

VI.B.25.166 [092 in *JJA*]

Note: Entries on this page are upside down.

(a) [r]**/Boy/ (I)**

Not located in MS/*FW*

(b) **Is scrubs floor**

(c) **had a certain complaint**

(d) **priv statem – mulier**

Note: ?Private statement.

L. *Mulier*. Woman.

(e) **inform obt from garage proprietor**

Note: Inform. obt. Information obtained.

(f) **milkfed**

(g) **scholars (scolar)**

(h) [o]**William ~~Shokkeeper~~ / Shopskeeper**

MS 47473-243, PrTMA: ^+[…] the man who had no notion of shopkeepers […]+^ | *JJA* 47:102 | Aug 1927 | I.6§1.4' | *FW* 128.16

(i) **Key's ring in matri**

Note: ?Matrimony.

(j) **1 fluid oz**

(k) [r]**eat his own length in / mackerel**

Daily News 28 July 1923-5/1: [Sands Hermits / Twelve-Egg Breakfast Man and Linguist Wife] After living for ten years under upturned boats and beneath fishermen's huts on the beach at the fishing station of Eastbourne, Philip Huggett, aged seventy-six, and his wife yesterday received notice to quit their

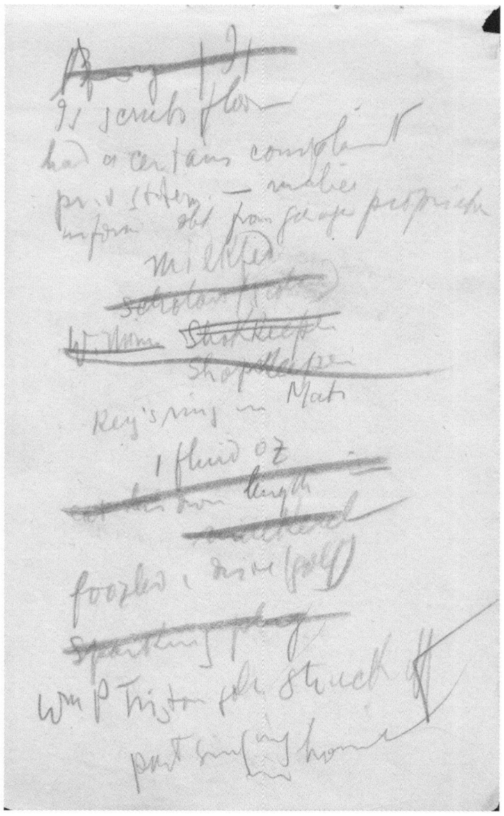

VI.B.25.166 [092 in *JJA*]

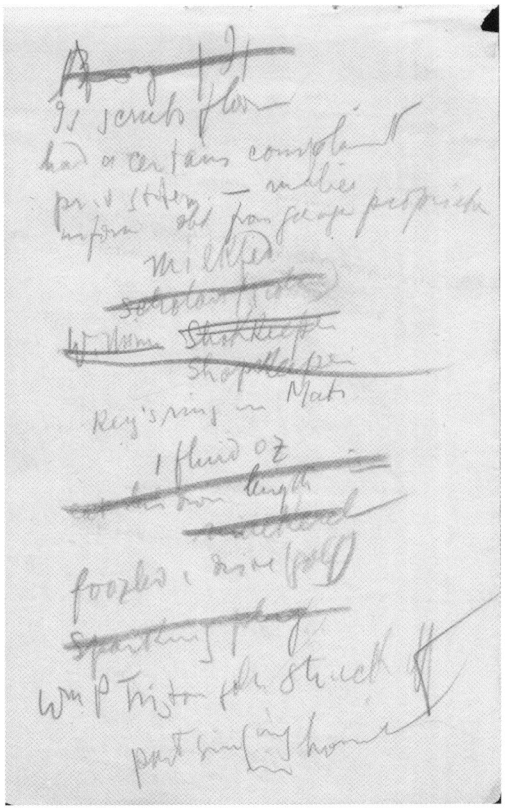

VI.B.25.166 [092 in *JJA*]

open air haunts, following a prosecution at the Police Court, where Huggett was fined 5*s*. for depositing material on the foreshore without the sanction of the council. The materials were tables and boxes of old iron, which constituted their effects. Huggett boasts that he makes a breakfast of twelve eggs and can eat his own length in mackerel.
MS 47472-133, LMA: Earwicker ^+, who previous to that semidetached life had been known to eat his own length in rainbow trout,+^ was ^+, like the salmon of his ladderleap,+^ secretly feeding on his own misplaced fat. | *JJA* 46:023 | Dec 1923 | I.4§1A.*2 | *FW* 079.08

(l) **foozled a drive (golf)**
Note: Foozle. To bungle a stroke in golf.

(m) **[r]sparking plug**
MS 474481-95v, LMA: before the traditional 10 seconds were up ^+volatile+^ Brittany considerately allowed his farfamed ^+sparking plug+^ chokegrip to relax | *JJA* 56:011 | Apr 1923 | II.4§1.*1 | *FW* 396.28

(n) **W^{m} P Tristan solr struck off**
Freeman's Journal 28 July 1923-5/3: Solicitor Struck Off the Rolls [...] Court of Appeal [...] order that the name of William P. Tristan [7 Dame Street and Athy] be removed from the roll of solicitors.
Note: Also in the *Irish Times* 28 July 1923.

(o) **part singing / in home**

VI.B.25.167 [093 in *JJA*]

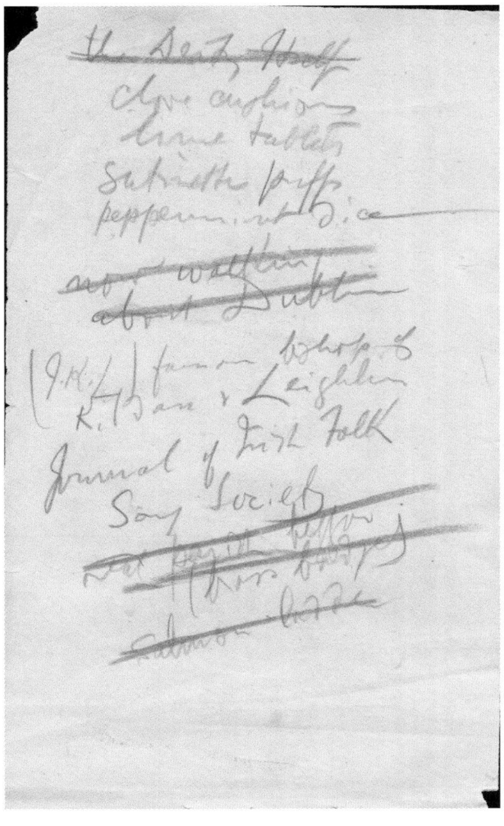

VI.B.25.167 [093 in *JJA*]

Note: Entries on this page are upside down.

(a) **[r]the Deity Itself**
MS 47471b-5, ILA: in the presence of the deity ^+Itself+^ | *JJA* 45:033 | Oct 1923 | I.2§2.*1 | *FW* 036.28

(b) **clove cushions >**

(c) **lime tablets >**

(d) **satinette puffs >**

(e) **peppermint dice**
Note: These appear to be manufacturer's names for sweets.

(f) **[b]now walking / about Dublin**
MS 47472-98v, ILA: ~~a man named Lyons~~ ^+quidam+^ ^+then walking about *Dublin* ^+with a bad record+^+^ | *JJA* 45:007 | Aug-Sep 1923 | *FW* 033.36-034.01

(g) **(J.K.L.) famous bishop of / Kildare & Leighlin**
Leader 28 Jul 1923-592/1: [The West Briton Defends Himself] I close with a quotation from the famous Bishop of Kildare and Leighlin (J.K.L.); "More depends on you than the will of Kings, or on the Acts of a Parliament. [...]"

(h) **Journal of Irish Folk / Song Society**
Leader 28 Jul 1923-597/1: [Journal of the Irish Folk Song Society] The latest number of the "Journal of the Irish Folk Society" [sic] is the 1923 number. It is volume six. It is a particularly good number. It contains eighteen Irish airs.

(i) **[r]real parish beggar / (brass badge)**
Leader 28 Jul 1923-597/2: [Journal of the Irish Folk Song Society] I find the

following note in the Editor's remarks. It is copied from the "Cork Archaeological Journal," 1898. It is a copy of an entry in Kilshannig Parish Vestry Book (Mallow, Co. Cork), for May 1745:— / "At a meeting of the inhabitants of Kilshannig, the following persons, and none other, are allowed to be common beggars of this parish, and to each of them a brass badge, marked 'Parish of Kilshannig,' was given to be publicly worn by said beggars to distinguish them from all Foreign Beggars."
MS 47471b-87, MT: a ~~brass badge~~ ^+a brazen nose & castiron mittens+^ for ~~Babbs~~ ~~Baby~~ ^+Babsy+^ ~~Beggar~~ ^+Beg+^ | *JJA* 48:031 | Feb 1924 | I.8§1A.*1/1B.*1 | [*FW* 210.12-13]

(j) **[r]salmon ladder**

Note: Salmon Ladder. See *OED*. A series of steps to enable salmon to ascend a fall or dam by a succession of leaps.
MS 47472-133, ILA: Earwicker ^+, who previous to that semidetached life had been known to eat his own length in rainbow trout,+^ was ^+, like the salmon of his ladderleap,+^ secretly feeding on his own misplaced fat | *JJA* 46:023 | Dec 1923 | I.4§1A.*2 | *FW* 079.11

VI.B.25.168 [094 in *JJA*]

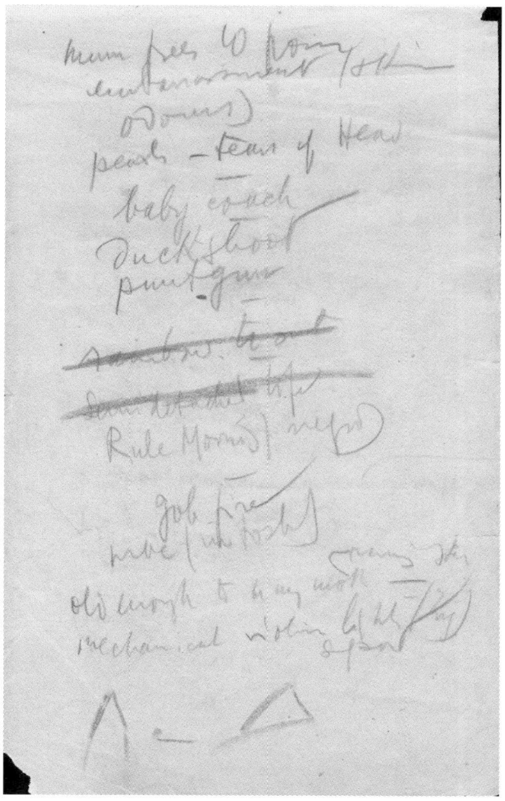

VI.B.25.168 [094 in *JJA*]

(a) **Mum frees W from / embarrassment (skin / odours)**

Note: Mum. Well-known deodorant. It first appeared in 19C America but was not produced in Britain until 1939.

(b) **pearls - tears of Heav**

(c) **baby coach**

(d) **duckshoot**

(e) **puntgun**

Note: Punt-gun. A gun used for shooting from a punt.

(f) **[r]rainbow trout**

MS 47472-133, LMA: Earwicker ^+, who previous to that semidetached life had been known to eat his own length in rainbow trout,+^ was ^+, like the salmon of his ladderleap,+^ secretly feeding on his own misplaced fat | *JJA* 46:023 | Dec 1923 | I.4§1A.*2 | *FW* 079.08

(g) **[r]semidetached life**

MS 47472-133, LMA: Earwicker ^+, who previous to that semidetached life had been known to eat his own length in rainbow trout,+^ was ^+, like the salmon of his ladderleap,+^ secretly feeding on his own misplaced fat | *JJA* 46:023 | Dec 1923 | I.4§1A.*2 | *FW* 079.06

(h) **Rule Mor/ning/ (negro)**

(i) **gob fire**

?Daily Mail 30 July 1923-7/7: ["Gob" Fire Disaster.] The worst colliery explosion has just happened in the South Yorkshire coalfield since the Cadeby disaster on July 9, 1912, occurred at the Maltby main colliery, seven miles from Rotherham, yesterday, and this afternoon all hope of saving the twenty-seven men who were in the affected area, has had to be abandoned [...] There have been what are called in the mining districts "gob" fires in the Maltby main pit for some time.
Note: Gob. In a mine, the empty space from which the coal has been extracted, but also the material used for packing such a space. A gob-fire is a fire

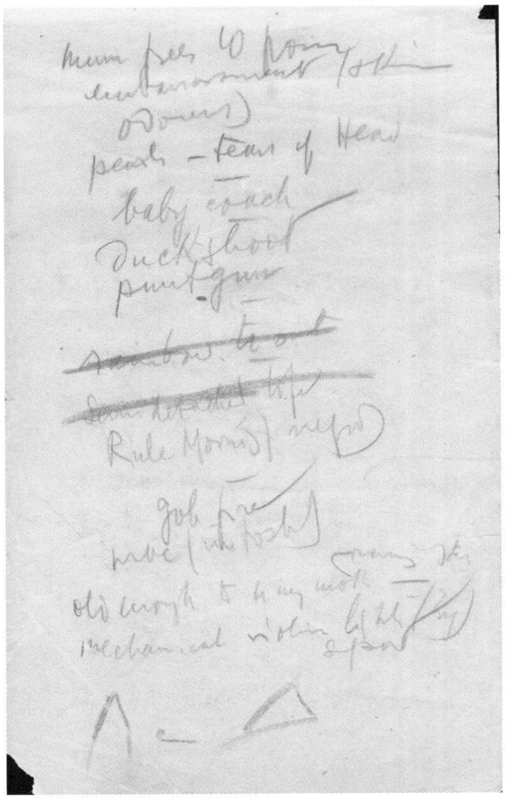

VI.B.25.168 [094 in *JJA*]

produced by the heat of the decomposing gob.

This story was widely reported: see also *Freeman's Journal* 30 July 4/4.

(j) **mac (in tosh)**

(k) **old enough to be my moth — ^+/rain sister/+^**

(l) **mechanical violin lights / sport } (Eng)**

(m) [+]**Λ c Δ**

Note: This entry is in red crayon. See colour reproduction at the end of this volume. See p. 4.

VI.B.25.169-70 [not in *JJA*] [blank]

VI.B.25.171 [095 in *JJA*] [blank]

VI.B.25.172 [096 in *JJA*]

VI.B.25.172 [096 in *JJA*]

Note: Entries on this page are upside down.

(a) [b]**voluntary poverty** >

MS 47488-25, MT: voluntarily poor Kevin | *JJA* 63:038c | Jul 1923 | IV§2.*2 | *FW* 605.06-7

(b) [b]**perpetual chastity** >

MS 47488-26, ILA: Kevin exorcised his holy sister water ^+, chaste perpetually,+^ | *JJA* 63:038d | Jul 1923 | IV§2.*3 | *FW* 606.01

(c) [b]**entire obedience** >

Note: See *CE* 'Christianity' 718a: To turn now to what is new in the moral teachings of Christ, we may say, once for all, that it embodied ethical perfection. There may be development of doctrine, but, after the Sermon on the Mount, there can be no further evolution of morals.[...] Christ taught the lesson of voluntary self-sacrifice. Never till His time were the Evangelical counsels — voluntary poverty, perpetual chastity, and entire obedience — preached or practised.

MS 47488-26, ILA: genuflecting ^+in entire obedience at ~~sextnoonon~~ ^+sextnoon+^+^ | *JJA* 63:038d | Jul 1923 | IV§2.*3 | *FW* 605.29

(d) [r]*[??]* **Water**

MS 47488-26, ILA: the regeneration of man by ^+affusion of+^ water. | *JJA* 63:038d | Jul 1923 | IV§2.*3 | *FW* 606.11-12

VI.B.25.173 [097 in *JJA*] [blank]

VI.B.25.174 [098 in *JJA*]

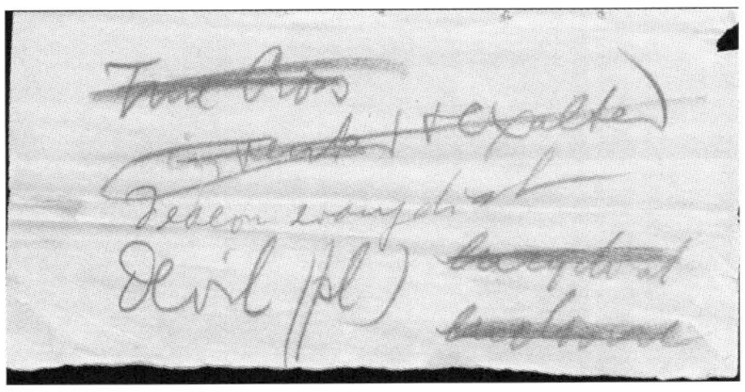

VI.B.25.174 [098 in *JJA*]

(a) [b]**True Cross / invented & exalted**

Note: The True Cross is the Cross on which Christ had been crucified. 'The Invention of the True Cross' refers to its discovery in 326, by Helena, the mother of the emperor Constantine. See *CE* 'Cross' 523.

MS 47488-25, ILA: when espousing the true cross ^+, invented & exalted,+^ in celibate matrimony | *JJA* 63:038c | Jul 1923 | IV§2.*2 | *FW* 605.09

(b) **deacon evangelical**

Note: Deacon evangelical. In non-conformist churches this is either an ordained or a lay preacher.

(c) **devil (pl)**

(d) [b]**encyclical**

MS 47488-25, ILA: Procreated on the ultimate island of Ireland in the ^+encyclical+^ Irish ocean | *JJA* 63:038c | Jul 1923 | IV§2.*2 | *FW* 000.00

(e) [b]**enclosure**

MS 47488-26, ILS: to build a ^+rubric+^ penitential honeybeehivehut ~~wherein~~ ^+in whose enclosure+^ to live in fortitude | *JJA* 63:038d | Jul 1923 | IV§2.*3 | *FW* 605.24

VI.B.25.175 [099 in *JJA*] [blank]

VI.B.25.176 [100 in *JJA*]

VI.B.25.176 [100 in *JJA*]

(a) **intention**

(b) **abtention**

Note: Abtention. The word does not appear in any of the standard dictionaries and has probably been constructed as an artificial antonym of 'intention'. Compare 178(a)-(b).

(c) **formal**

(d) **omnipollent**

Note: Omnipollent. All-powerful. See *U* 14.16 (the only citation given by the *OED* for this word).

(e) [b]**violet >**

MS 47488-26, ILA: water whereamid ^+when violet vesper tell+^ Saint Kevin | *JJA* 63:038d | Jul 1923 | IV§2.*3 | *FW* 606.04

(f) [b]**white >**

MS 47488-25, ILA: feast of precreated holy ^+whiteclad+^ angels | *JJA* 63:038c | Jul 1923 | IV§2.*2 | *FW* 605.06

(g) [b]**red >**

MS 47488-26, ILA: to build a ^+rubric+^ penitential honeybeehivehut | *JJA* 63:038d | Jul 1923 | IV§2.*3 | *FW* 605.23

(h) [b]**green >**

MS 47488-25, ILA: midmost Glendalough ^+le Vert+^ by archangelical guidance | *JJA* 63:038c | Jul 1923 | IV§2.*2 | *FW* 605.11

(i) [b]**black**

Note: Entries (e)-(i) comprise a list of the liturgical colours worn by the priest and used to dress the altar on certain feast days of the Church.
MS 47488-26, LMS: having girded his ~~frock~~ ^+^+~~candid alb~~ ^+sable+^+^ cappa magna+^ | *JJA* 63:038d | Jul 1923 | IV§2.*3 | *FW* 606.05

(j) [b]**Matins ~ >**

MS 47488-25, ILA: when espousing the true cross ^+, invented & exalted,+^ in celibate matrimony, ^+at matin chime+^ arose | *JJA* 63:038c | Jul 1923 |

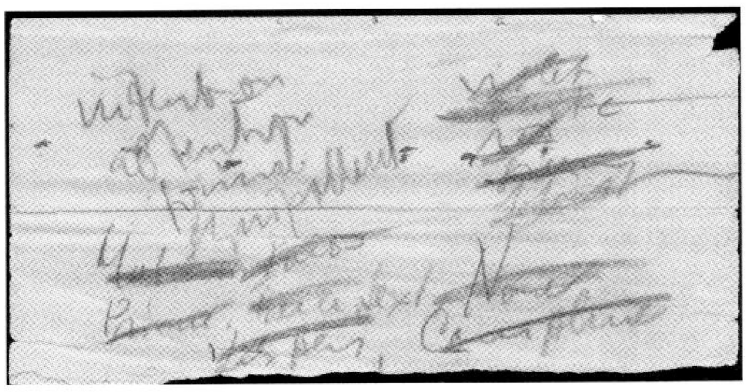

VI.B.25.176 [100 in *JJA*]

VI.B.25.176 is reproduced in colour at the end of this volume

IV§2.*2 | *FW* 605.09

(k) **[b]Lauds >**

MS 47488-25, LMA: piously Kevin ^+lauding the Triune Trishagion,+^ | *JJA* 63:038c | Jul 1923 | IV§2.*2 | *FW* 605.14

(l) **[b]Prime, ~ >**

MS 47488-26, LMS: whereon ^+by ~~the hour of~~ prime+^, | *JJA* 63:038d | Jul 1923 | IV§2.*3 | *FW* 605.18

(m) **[b]Terce, ~ >**

MS 47488-26, ILA: holy Kevin bided ^+till the third ^+morn+^ hour+^ but to build a ^+rubric+^ penitential honeybeehivehut | *JJA* 63:038d | Jul 1923 | IV§2.*3 | *FW* 605.23

(n) **[b]Sext, ~ >**

MS 47488-26, ILA: genuflecting ^+in entire obedience at ~~sextnoonon~~ ^+sextnoon+^+^ | *JJA* 63:038d | Jul 1923 | IV§2.*3 | *FW* 605.30

(o) **[b]None >**

MS 47488-26, ILA: most blessed Kevin ^+ninthly+^ enthroned | *JJA* 63:038d | Jul 1923 | IV§2.*3 | *FW* 606.03

(p) **[b]Vespers, ~ >**

MS 47488-26, ILA: water whereamid ^+when violet vesper tell+^ Saint Kevin | *JJA* 63:038d | Jul 1923 | IV§2.*3 | *FW* 606.04

(q) **[b]Compline**

Note: Entries (j)-(q) make up a list of the canonical hours, the various parts of the Divine Office of the Church which are appointed for different hours of the day.
MS 47488-26, BMS: ~~solemnly~~ ^+at solemn compline+^ sat in his seat of wisdom | *JJA* 63:038d | Jul 1923 | IV§2.*3 | *FW* 606.06

VI.B.25.177 [101 in *JJA*] [blank]

VI.B.25.178 [102 in *JJA*]

VI.B.25.178 [102 in *JJA*]

VI.B.25.178 is reproduced in colour at the end of this volume

Note: Entries on this page are upside down.

(a) **[b]precreated >**

MS 47488-25, ILA: come his feast of ^+precreated+^ holy angels | *JJA* 63:038c | Jul 1923 | IV§2.*2 | *FW* 605.05

(b) **[b]postcreated**

Note: Precreated; postcreated. These terms derive from the unresolved debate within the Church as to whether the creation of the angels preceded or followed the creation of the heavens and all material things (a further possibility is that God created them simul ab initio temporis – at the same time from the beginning). The only *OED* citation for 'postcreation' is *U* 14.296.
MS 47488-25, LMA: privilege of a ^+postcreated+^ priest's portable altar | *JJA* 63:038c | Jul 1923 | IV§2.*2 | *FW* 605.08

(c) **[b]*[??]*ian**

(d) [b]*[??]*

(e) [b]*[??]*

VI.B.25.179-83 [not in *JJA*] [blank]

VI.B.25.184 [not in *JJA*]

(a) *[??]***wc)**
Note: This entry is sideways.

VI.B.25.185-92 [not in *JJA*] [blank]

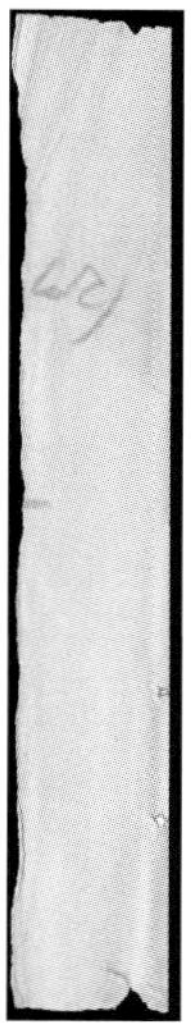

VI.B.25.184 [not in *JJA*]
(sideways)

Appendices

I. Table of usage in *Finnegans Wake*

***FW* reference**	**UNIT**	**VI.B.25 reference**
FW 017.20	[r]Saltings	VI.B.25.155(f)
FW 020.19	[r]Fly not yet	VI.B.25.158(c)
FW 023.16	[r]culprit	VI.B.25.017(a)
FW 031.07	[b]paternoster (bait)	VI.B.25.031(a)
FW 031.20	[b]an Italian Excellency	VI.B.25.149(h)
FW 032.13	[b]holograph	VI.B.25.144(l)
FW 033.30	[b]throughout my existence	VI.B.25.160(f)
FW 033.36-034.01	[b]now walking / about Dublin	VI.B.25.167(f)
FW 034.04	[b]Vigilance Committee	VI.B.25.033(a)
FW 034.13	[b]Southron	VI.B.25.160(g)
FW 036.24	[r]sign of our redemption	VI.B.25.164(k)
FW 036.28	the Deity Itself	VI.B.25.167(a)
FW 039.01	[r]boys' 1d flutter	VI.B.25.151(h)
FW 039.16	[r]out of pawn (prison)	VI.B.25.150(p)
FW 040.15	[r]Cash draper	VI.B.25.160(c)
FW 042.29-30	[r]young Dublin	VI.B.25.151(I)
FW 049.11	[r]saw him no more	VI.B.25.143(j)
FW 049.23	[r]passed away to the Beyond / by means of poison	VI.B.25.149(j)
FW 050.23	[r]sinning society	VI.B.25.126(a)
FW 051.02	[r]passing of	VI.B.25.154(m)
FW 059.25	[r]Ginger Jane / (car)	VI.B.25.155(c)
FW 059.25	[r]a runabout	VI.B.25.157(b)
FW 060.05	[r]a crying shame	VI.B.25.163(e)
FW 062.28	[r]humping a *[*passport*]*	VI.B.25.157(a)
FW 063.28	[r]gatepier	VI.B.25.164(i)
FW 070.33-4	[r]luncheonette	VI.B.25.148(a)
FW 079.06	[r]semidetached life	VI.B.25.168(a)
FW 079.08	[r]eat his own length in / mackerel	VI.B.25.166(k)
FW 079.08	[r]rainbow trout	VI.B.25.168(f)
FW 079.11	[r]salmon ladder	VI.B.25.167(j)
FW 079.11-12	[r]Salmon Leap	VI.B.25.152(e)
FW 098.20	[r]drowned in a pond while / intoxicated	VI.B.25.164(d)
FW 099.27	[r]There has been murder	VI.B.25.152(l)
FW 108.28	[r]dinkum	VI.B.25.156(j)
FW 108.28	[r]give me the dinkum / oil	VI.B.25.157(a)
FW 117.23	[r]3 jeers	VI.B.25.150(n)

FW 128.16	[o]William Shopskeeper	VI.B.25.166(h)
FW 172.02	[r]florist	VI.B.25.021(a)
FW 173.26	[r]3 jeers	VI.B.25.150(n)
FW 174.10	[r]as I simply agree / to it	VI.B.25.150(j)
FW 176.26	[r]got the better of	VI.B.25.160(h)
FW 177.07	[r]his trousers changed / colour	VI.B.25.160(a)
FW 177.16	[r]mental defective	VI.B.25.165(b)
FW 179.20	[r]drunkery	VI.B.25.157(e)
FW 180.34	[r]bumpersprinkling	VI.B.25.159(g)
FW 187.01	[r]skittled out	VI.B.25.149(f)
[*FW* 201.35]	[r]O laws!	VI.B.25.160(m)
FW 205.29	[r]Pat the Man	VI.B.25.150(a)
FW 206.35	[g]Usher's Isl	VI.B.25.154(k)
FW 210.02	[r]Pop (Maundy)	VI.B.25.153(a)
FW 210.11	[r]Needles & Pins / Blankets & Skins / When a man's married / His sorrow begins	VI.B.25.165(a)
FW 210.12-13	[r]real parish beggar / (brass badge)	VI.B.25.167(I)
FW 210.13	[r]saints *[??]* / — stripes	VI.B.25.142(a)
FW 210.14	Kevineen	VI.B.25.153(b)
FW 381.21	[b]decorated by most / regal of belches	VI.B.25.162(d)
FW 383.20	[r]as slow their ship	VI.B.25.159(h)
FW 386.01	[r]Nature embellished / the tint	VI.B.25.158(a)
FW 390.36	[b]fullbottom wig	VI.B.25.155(a)
FW 393.26	[b]Kookaburra bell	VI.B.25.157(p)
FW 395.16	[r]rosecrumpler	VI.B.25.159(e)
FW 395.26	[r]a pretty thing happened	VI.B.25.145(i)
FW 396.11-12	[r]most unholy blue	VI.B.25.159(f)
FW 396.22	[r]heaven knows	VI.B.25.158(e)
FW 396.28	[r]sparking plug	VI.B.25.166(n)
FW 396.29	[r]volatile	VI.B.25.164(e)
FW 398.20	[r]dimpling bliss	VI.B.25.159(a)
FW 412.14	[r]incensed (Kev)	VI.B.25.153(d)
FW 430.22	[r]one rosy Smile	VI.B.25.158(k)
FW 451.34	[r]first class!	VI.B.25.163(f)
FW 455.25-6	[r]the pleasure of the morrow	VI.B.25.149(i)
FW 461.36	[r]gloriously kind	VI.B.25.157(m)
FW 472.25	*[How]* grateful should / be For he it was / that said if God said / [r]may I say it— / offence, I rarely / *[hear]* service / in one man	VI.B.25.146(i)

FW 472.32	^{r}the Spirit above	VI.B.25.158(b)
FW 532.17-18	^{r}keep my wicket up	VI.B.25.149(k)
FW 533.24	^{r}as you all know	VI.B.25.149(l)
FW 533.25f	^{r}one of the ambitions of / my early youth (SP) I was / confirmed in bed	VI.B.25.149(m)
FW 539.21-2	^{r}ran selection	VI.B.25.157(k)
FW 562.36	^{b}how unpardonable of me!	VI.B.25.162(f)
FW 564.06-8	^{g}command a full / view	VI.B.25.153(j)
FW 566.07	^{r}in ? mourning	VI.B.25.162(I)
FW 605.05	^{b}precreated	VI.B.25.178(a)
FW 605.06	^{b}white	VI.B.25.176(f)
FW 605.06-7	^{b}voluntary poverty	VI.B.25.172(a)
FW 605.08	^{b}postcreated	VI.B.25.178(b)
FW 605.09	^{b}True Cross / invented & exalted	VI.B.25.174(a)
FW 605.09	^{b}Matins	VI.B.25.176(j)
FW 605.11	^{b}green	VI.B.25.176(h)
FW 605.14	^{b}Lauds	VI.B.25.176(k)
FW 605.18	^{b}Prime	VI.B.25.176(l)
FW 605.23	^{b}red	VI.B.25.176(g)
FW 605.23	^{b}Terce	VI.B.25.176(m)
FW 605.24	^{b}enclosure	VI.B.25.174(e)
FW 605.29	^{b}entire obedience	VI.B.25.172(c)
FW 605.30	^{r}collected water / continuously	VI.B.25.154(j)
FW 605.30	^{b}Sext	VI.B.25.176(n)
FW 606.01	^{b}perpetual chastity	VI.B.25.172(b)
FW 606.03	^{b}None	VI.B.25.176(o)
FW 606.04	^{b}violet	VI.B.25.176(e)
FW 606.04	^{b}Vespers	VI.B.25.176(p)
FW 606.05	^{b}black	VI.B.25.176(i)
FW 606.06	^{b}Compline	VI.B.25.176(q)
FW 606.07-8	^{r}doc universal ch	VI.B.25.154(e)
FW 606.09	^{r}extempore prayer	VI.B.25.154(h)
FW 606.11-12	^{r}*[??]* Water	VI.B.25.172(a)
FW 615.27	^{r}swags	VI.B.25.157(h)
FW 618.20	^{r}treated not very grand	VI.B.25.145(a)
FW 618.36-619.01	biz v pleasure	VI.B.25.018(b)
FW 618.36-619.01	^{r}professionaly known *[as]*	VI.B.25.152(m)

II. *First Draft Version* index

FDV reference	UNIT	VI.B.25 reference
FDV 059.21	^{r}culprit	VI.B.25.017(a)
FDV 065.03	^{r}boys' 1d flutter	VI.B.25.151(h)
FDV 069.07	^{r}passed away *[to]* the Beyond / by means of poison	VI.B.25.149(j)
FDV 069.13	^{r}?*[sinning society]*	VI.B.25.126(a)
FDV 069.20	^{r}passing of	VI.B.25.154(m)
FDV 079.29	^{r}drowned in a pond while / intoxicated	VI.B.25.164(d)
FDV 081.14	^{r}swags	VI.B.25.157(h)
FDV 082.33	^{r}treated not very grand	VI.B.25.145(a)
FDV 082.35	^{r}[pull a gun]	VI.B.25.139(a)
FDV 082.38	^{r}perfectly proud of *[??]*	VI.B.25.129(a)
FDV 083.08	^{r}(signed)	VI.B.25.150(k)
FDV 085.10	^{r}dinkum	VI.B.25.156(j)
FDV 085.10	^{r}give me the dinkum / oil	VI.B.25.157(n)
FDV 089.13	^{r}professionaly known *[as]*	VI.B.25.152(m)
FDV 110.20-1	^{r}as I *[simply]* agree / to it	VI.B.25.150(j)
FDV 111.02	^{r}his trousers changed / colour	VI.B.25.160(a)
FDV 111.14	^{r}mental defective	VI.B.25.165(b)
FDV 111.31	^{r}florist	VI.B.25.021(a)
FDV 116.27	^{r}drunkery	VI.B.25.157(e)
FDV 116.38	^{r}bumpersprinkling	VI.B.25.159(g)
FDV 119.10	^{r}skittled out	VI.B.25.149(f)
FDV 120.16	^{r}deliciae meae	VI.B.25.143(d)
FDV 127.14	^{r}Pop (Maundy)	VI.B.25.153(a)
FDV 127.18	^{r}Needles & Pins / Blankets & Skins / When a man's married / His sorrow begins	VI.B.25.165(a)
FDV 127.19-20	^{r}real parish beggar / (brass badge)	VI.B.25.167(i)
FDV 127.22	^{r}saints *[??]* / stripes	VI.B.25.142(a)
FDV 127.22	Kevineen	VI.B.25.153(b)
FDV 204.03	^{b}decorated by most / regal of belches	VI.B.25.162(d)
FDV 215.09	^{b}fullbottom wig	VI.B.25.155(a)
FDV 276.04	Kevineen	VI.B.25.153(b)

III. A Selective List of Sources and Topics

Colour reproductions

Top fold, centre fold, openings 148-149, 156-157, 158-159, 162-163, page 155, fragments of pages 108-109, 120, 126, 176, 178.

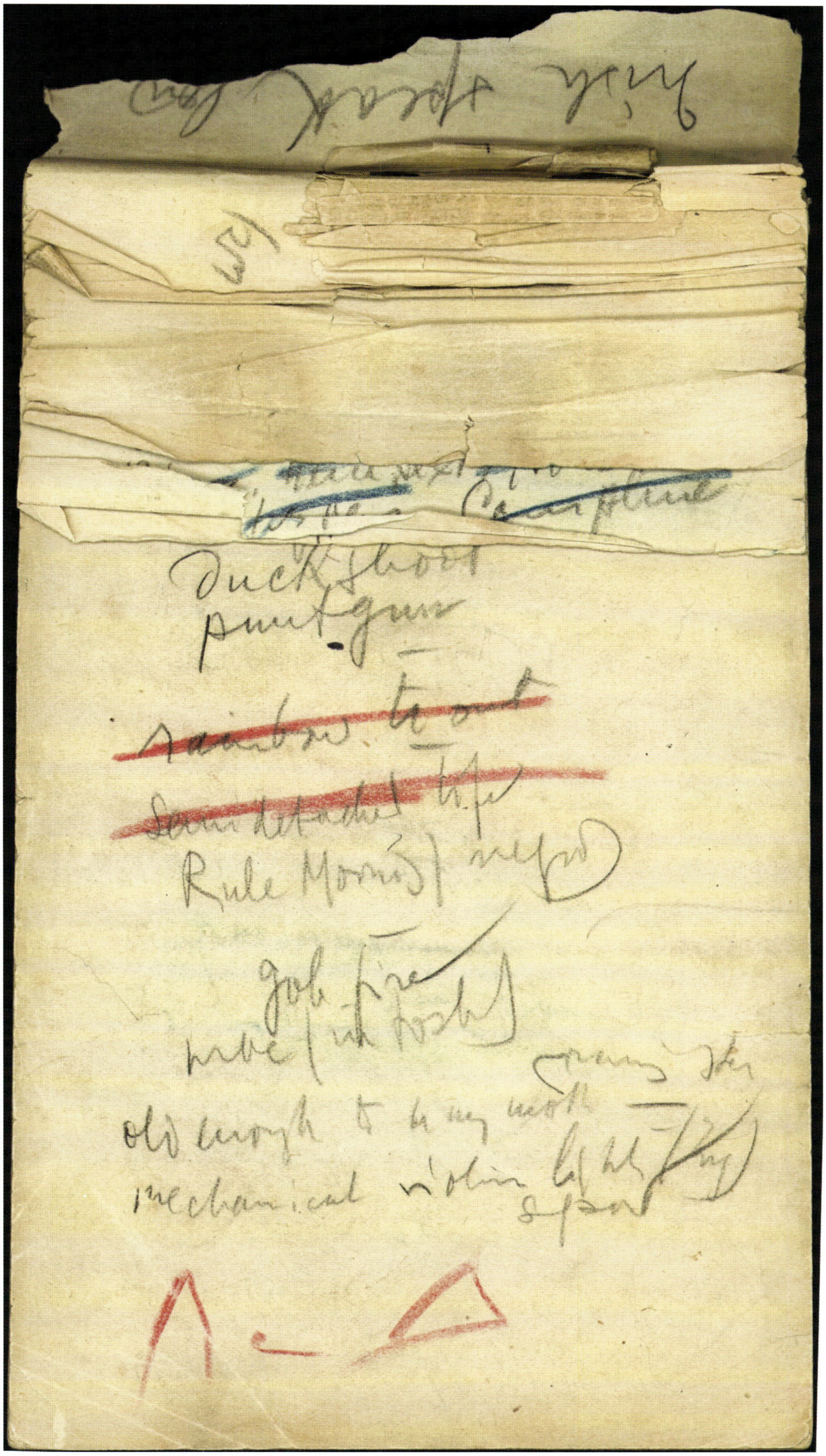

VI.B.25: top fold.
The first page (upside-down) and the last pages.
The intact page bearing the red sigla is VI.B.25.168.

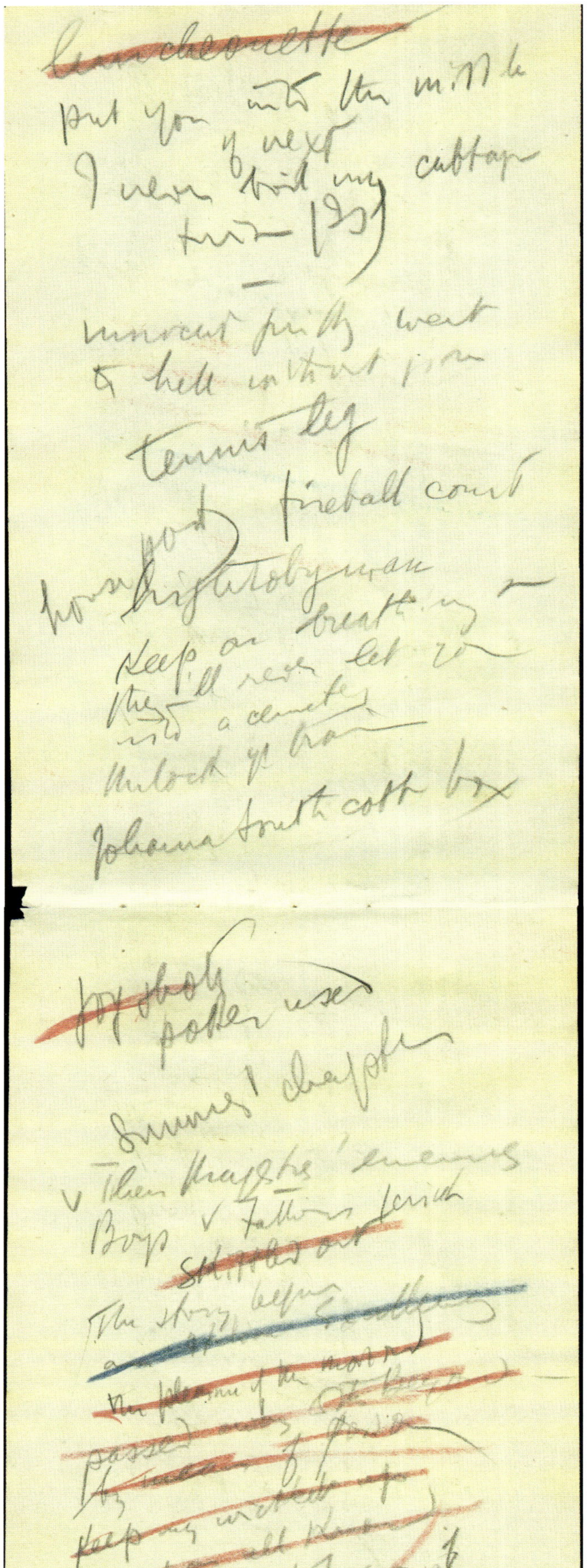

VI.B.25.148-149

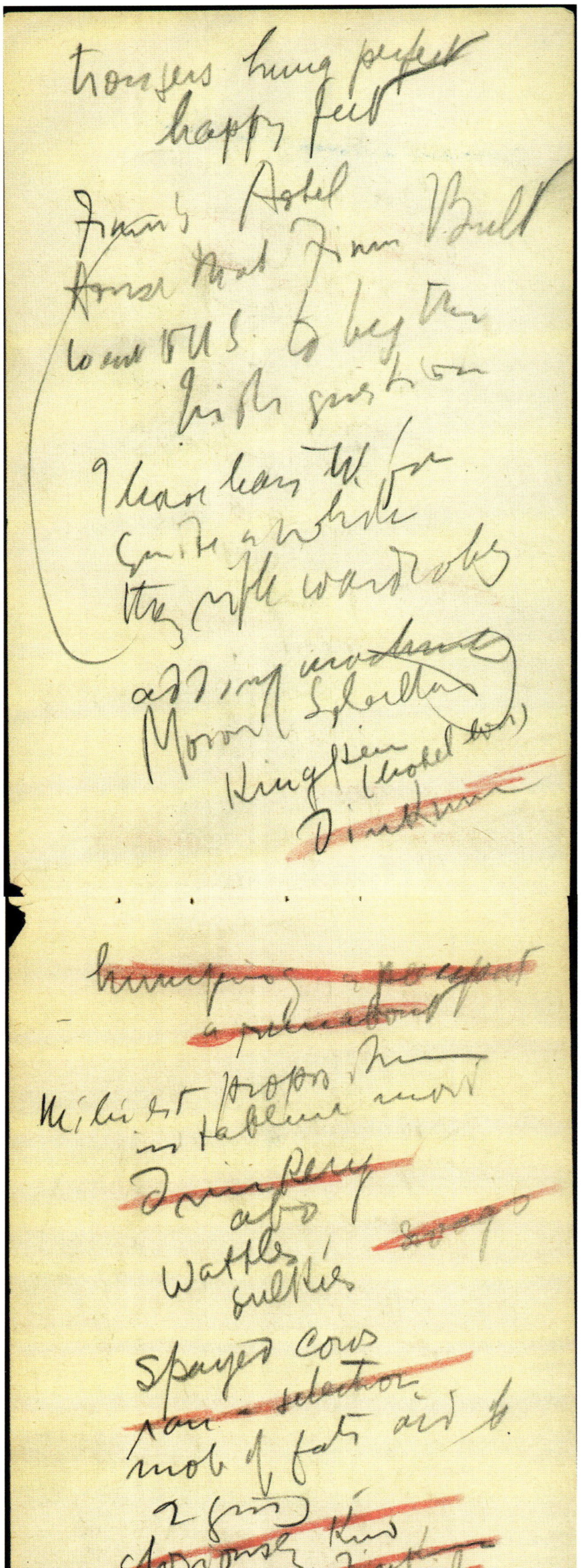

VI.B.25.156-157

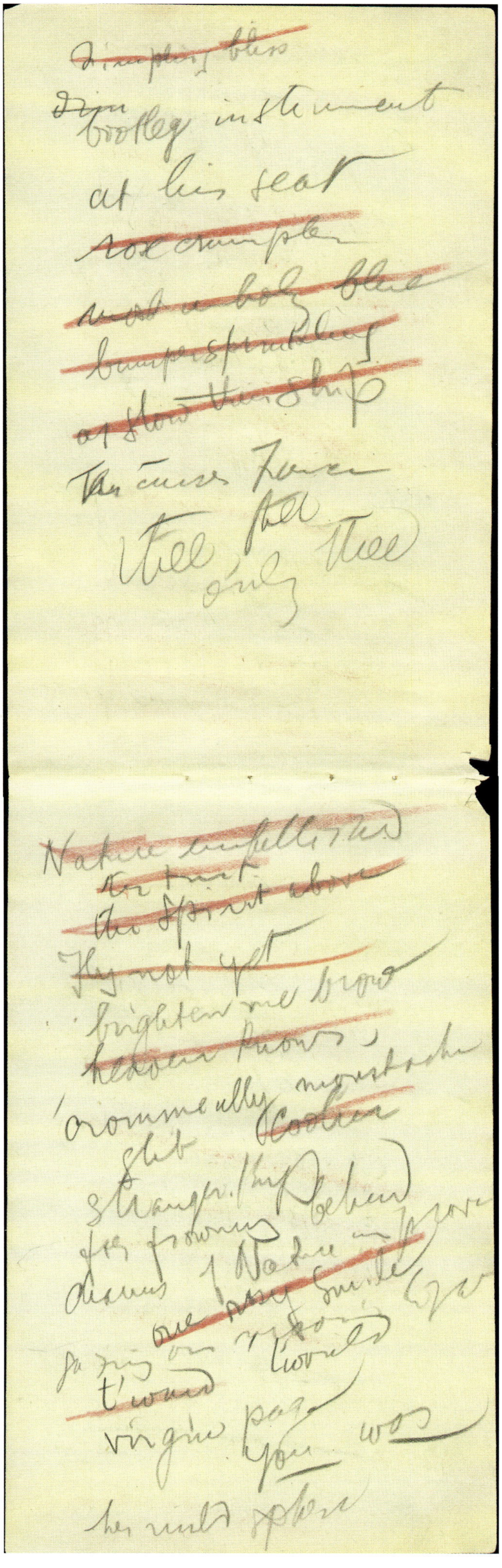

VI.B.25.158-159 upside down

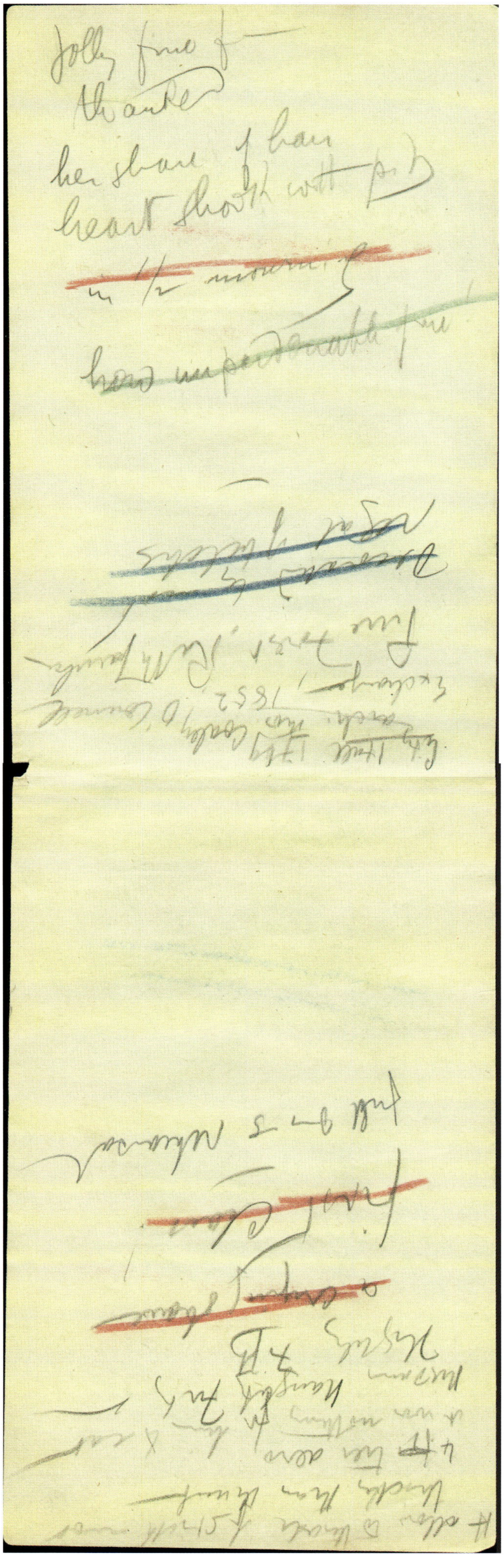

VI.B.25.162-163

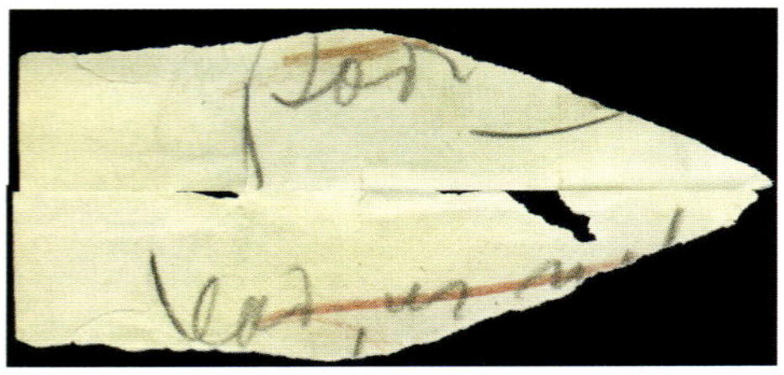

VI.B.25.108-109

VI.B.25.120

VI.B.25.126

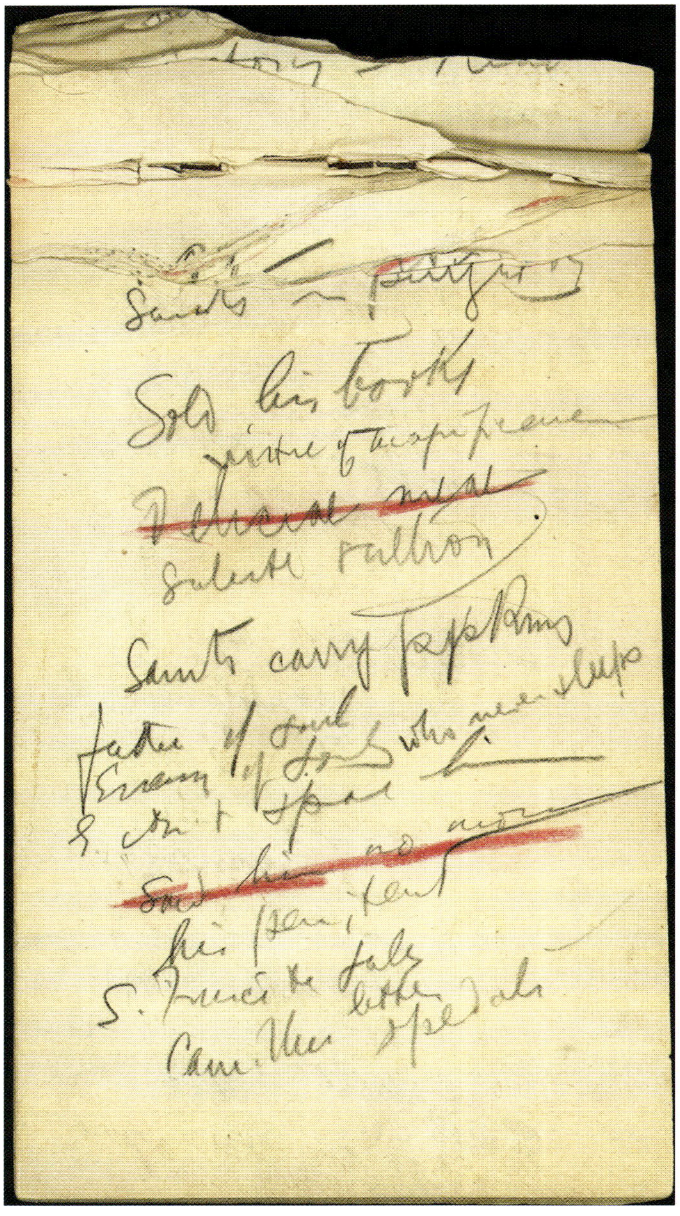

Centre fold
The intact page is VI.B.25.143

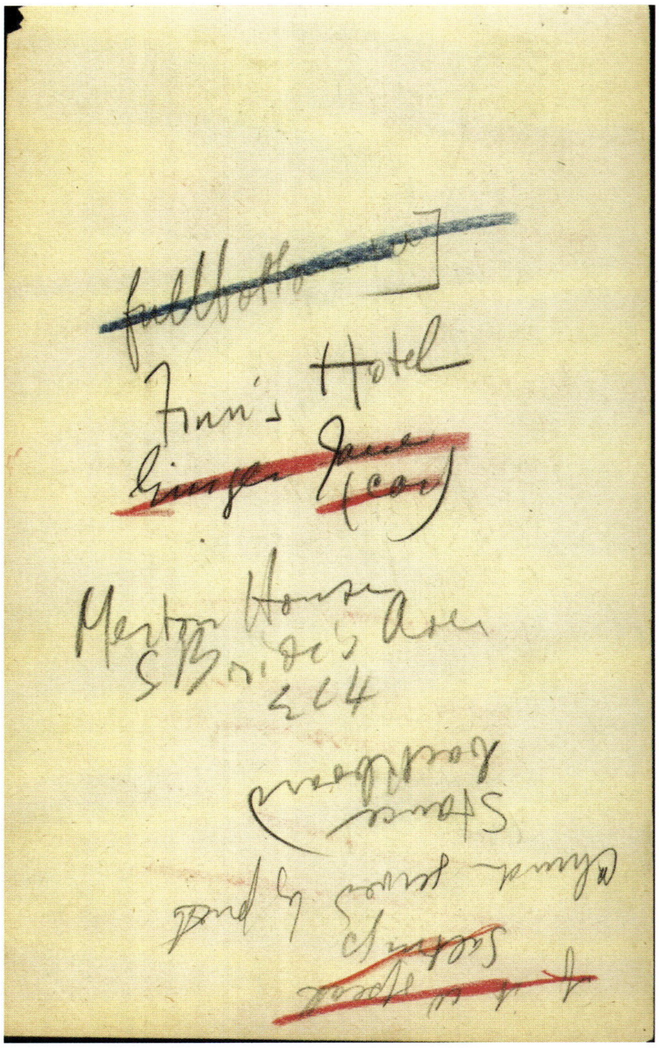

VI.B.25.155

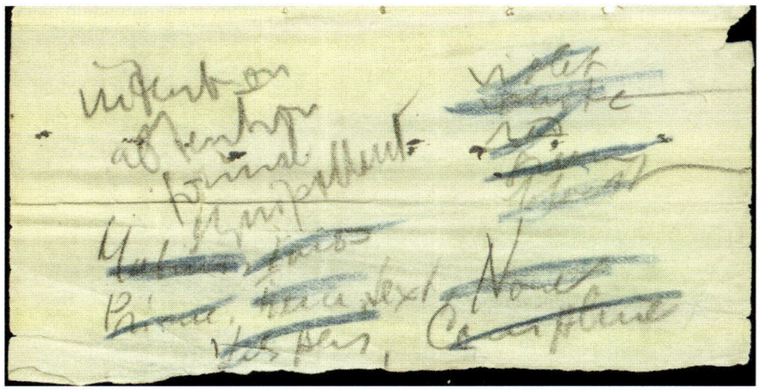

VI.B.25.176

VI.B.25.178